Tennessee
OFF THE BEATEN PATH

"Whether you're a native or just planning a vacation to Tennessee, this book is a must for anyone who has occasion to drive in the state."
—*Southern RV*

"O'Brien skillfully scouts out its musical heritage, delta plains, miniature golf sites, and the best catfish restaurant anywhere!"
—*Bookpage*

"Provides in-depth focus, offering a survey of regional history, local attractions and recommendations which would not be seen in a more general Southern guide. Highly recommended."
—*Midwest Book Review*

"Designed for travelers who like to taste the true flavor of a state."
—*Southern Living*

To my parents, Jim and Ann, for instilling in me the wanderlust that has always given me the desire to travel the world's least-traveled byways.

TENNESSEE

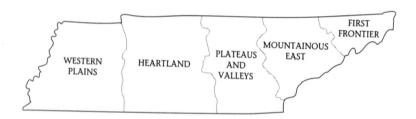

WESTERN PLAINS

HEARTLAND

PLATEAUS AND VALLEYS

MOUNTAINOUS EAST

FIRST FRONTIER

Contents

The Lookout Mountain Incline Railway, Chattanooga

Introduction

The state of Tennessee is a fun state to explore. From the mountainous areas in the east to the delta plains of the Mississippi River in the west, the variety of natural wonders and attractions the state has to offer is awesome.

It would take volumes to detail all of Tennessee's highlights. In *Tennessee: Off the Beaten Path*, we've narrowed your choice down considerably by taking you off the interstates and onto the side roads, where the character of the state shines through.

The state is an easy one to get around in. Major highways and interstates are abundant, and even though you won't be spending much time on those behemoths, it's nice to know they're there if you have to make a quick escape back to civilization.

The Tennessee Scenic Parkway System covers 2,300 miles of primarily two-lane roads that connect the state's parks, major lakes, historical sites, recreational attractions, and this book's lesser-known attractions. The parkways are marked with a sign sporting a mockingbird, the state bird. They are mounted directly above the state highway designation numbers along the roads at key intersections.

If you follow the suggestions in this book, you'll find yourself driving up steep mountain roads, across rolling plains, over a few century-old bridges, and down many a gravel road. You'll also find yourself floating on a lake 300 feet below the earth's surface, playing miniature golf on the side of a mountain, and eating the world's sweetest-tasting, vilest-smelling vegetable.

As in any area with a great deal of tourist traffic, Tennessee has its share of tourist traps along the well-worn trails. Sometimes our trip down the less-traveled paths of the state will intersect with those trails in order to highlight an event, an attraction, or a person worth visiting. We have found that sometimes it's worth fighting a crowd to see something that we'll probably never get a chance to see again. You'll find many of those once-in-a-lifetime opportunities in Tennessee.

Music is a big attraction in the state. From the birthplace of the blues in Memphis to the birthplace of the Grand Ole Opry in Nashville to the songs of the Appalachian Mountain folk, music of all kinds has played an important part in the heritage of Tennessee. Our tour of the state will touch on much of that heritage and the people who have contributed to it. We'll visit the commercial monuments that honor Carl Perkins, Dolly Parton, Loretta Lynn, Conway Twitty, and many others.

Southern hospitality is more than a myth in Tennessee, and our people may well be the state's friendliest attraction. There is one thing you'll never have to worry about as you travel through the state: You'll never truly be lost. Knock on any door or stop by any store, and chances are you'll get the directions you need, plus a whole lot more. Just when you think you've met the world's most colorful person, you'll meet one just a bit more fun. That's the way it is in Tennessee.

The state is full of crossroad communities with colorful and descriptive names. Usually, the community has little more to offer than a gas station–general store combination, but here's where you'll usually find the most intriguing characters of the area.

In the summer, these folks will be sitting on the porch of that store solving the world's problems. In the winter, you'll find them sitting around the pot-bellied stove. There are more than a hundred such communities around the state with colorful names, including Fly, New Flys Village, Defeated Creek, Ugly Creek, Pretty Creek, Dull, Soddy-Daisy, Bell Buckle, Gilt Edge, Finger, Frogjump, Nutbush, Bucksnort, Only, Who'd A Thought It, and Skullbone.

For tourism promotion purposes, state officials have divided the state into five major areas:

The First Frontier. More than 200 years ago, this part of the state was America's new frontier. Explorers, including Daniel Boone, blazed paths across the Appalachian Mountains, establishing some of the first settlements outside the original thirteen colonies.

Much of the area is heavily forested, with the extreme east and southern parts quite mountainous. Davy Crockett was born here, and the state of Franklin, which never quite made it to statehood, was formed here several years before Tennessee became a state.

The Mountainous East. As the name implies, this area is probably the most rugged of all Tennessee terrain. The 500,000-acre Great Smoky Mountain National Park and its foothill communities provide beauty incomparable to what you'll find elsewhere in the Southeast.

Throughout the area several museums have dedicated their collections and grounds to the preservation of mountain life, and many communities have preserved that life-style by their very existence.

Plateaus and Valleys. Forested and rugged, the Cumberland

Plateau rises like a gigantic wall that spans the width of the state, forming the western boundary of the Tennessee Valley.

Although relatively flat, the area has many spectacular streams that have carved out deep gorges in the sandstone, making it one of the best areas in the state for white-water enthusiasts.

The Heartland. Also known as Middle Tennessee, the area is a region of gently rolling hills, sloping green meadows, and miles of river and lake frontage.

At the heart of the area lies Nashville, "Music City USA," the home of the Grand Ole Opry. Musical attractions are popular in this area, as are Tennessee Walking Horse farms, sour mash whiskey distilleries, and the homes of two U.S. presidents.

Western Plains. An area of fertile bottomlands and dense hardwood forests, the Western Plains is bordered on the east by the Tennessee River and on the west by the Mississippi.

A few of the state's most colorful folk heroes, frontiersman Davy Crockett, train engineer Casey Jones, and *Walking Tall* sheriff Buford Pusser, have strong roots here, as do *Roots* author Alex Haley and the King of Rock 'n' Roll, Elvis Presley.

The 520-mile-long state is divided into two telephone area codes, 901 and 615, and about half of it lies in the eastern time zone and half in the central zone.

While care has been taken to ensure accuracy in all listings in this book, visitors would be advised to call ahead before traveling any great distance. Life throughout Tennessee is slow paced and mellow, so if a day appears to be going a bit slow, it isn't uncommon for a proprietor to close early and go fishing. Phone numbers have been included in listings where appropriate.

Most of the attractions are open on a year-round basis, but some cut operations a bit during the winter months.

Before venturing forth, you may want to contact the state tourism bureau and load up on brochures and maps of the areas you plan on visiting. In the material you receive from the state, there will be a list of local tourism bureaus that will be able to provide even more specific information.

Write to Tennessee Tourist Development, P.O. Box 23170, Nashville, TN 37202, or call (615) 741–2158.

Note: Because of periodic price increases, admission prices to individual attractions have not been listed. The publisher recommends that readers call attractions before traveling to obtain current information.

Off the Beaten Path on the First Frontier

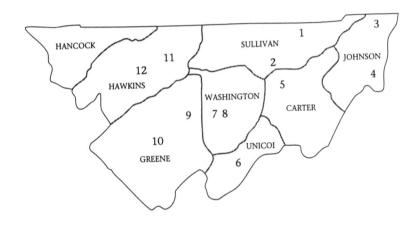

1. The Grand Guitar Museum
2. Ridgewood Restaurant
3. Iron Mountain Stoneware
4. Trade
5. The Kissing Bridge
6. Erwin
7. Old Town Hall
8. Parson's Table Restaurant
9. Davy Crockett Birthplace
   State Historical Area
10. Tusculum College
11. Tennessee Mountaineer
    Restaurant
12. Hale Springs Inn

The First Frontier

Sullivan County

Bristol is about as far north as one can go in the state and stay in Tennessee. In fact, about half the city is in Virginia. The state line runs down the middle of State Street in the heart of the downtown shopping district. But other than the small state markers embedded in the street between the double yellow lines, there's little evidence that the city has two mayors, two city councils, and two telephone area codes.

A big, old-fashioned neon sign forms an archway across State Street, near Randall Street, and proclaims "Bristol is a good place to live." Arrows point to the Tennessee and Virginia sides.

Although Nashville, about 300 miles to the west, gets credit for being the center of country music, it was here in Bristol that the Carter Family and Jimmie Rodgers recorded the first country-and-western music that was distributed nationwide. That recording took place on August 2, 1927, and put the area on the musical map. A monument honoring those musical pioneers stands at Edgemont Avenue and State Street. Farther down State Street, a large mural on the side of a building presents a visual memorial to that event.

Continue down State Street and take a right on Common-wealth Avenue. In about three blocks is an area known as the Commonwealth Antique Section. There, you'll find an antique mall and about a half-dozen other similar shops.

In keeping with the musical heritage of the area, ⊃**The Grand Guitar Museum** is located at 535 New Kingsport Highway. Follow State Street out of downtown, and you'll see the museum in about 3¹/₂ miles, on the right. (The street turns into New Kingsport Highway once you leave downtown.) The building is built to resemble a guitar lying on its side and is said to be the only guitar-shaped building in the world. Inside are several displays of rare stringed instruments and a gift shop. Open weekends only; admission charged; (615) 968–2277.

In nearby Kingsport, early travelers through the area exchanged their Virginia currency for Tennessee money at a stagecoach stop known as the **Exchange Place.** Today, the small farmlike village and crafts center is open Thursday through Sunday during

The Grand Guitar Museum

the warmer months. You'll usually find a group of ladies working on a quilt outside under one of the large shade trees. The village is located just off Highway 11W, at 4812 Orebank Road. Admission free; (615) 288–6071.

Unlikely as it seems, a major U.S. boatyard was in operation along the Holston River here in Kingsport in 1802. William King's boatyard had a quality reputation that stretched as far as New Orleans. On the hill across the stagecoach road from the yards was the always-busy **Netherland Inn,** an inn and tavern where the likes of the state's three presidents, Andrew Jackson, Andrew Johnson, and James K. Polk, whiled away hours with their friends. The inn has been restored and is open to the public as a museum. Several other buildings on the property, including a shop and wagon shelter, have also been restored. A log cabin that was moved here from Virginia and once served as Daniel Boone's home from 1773 to 1775 is now a children's museum; it is a must if there are any small travelers with you. The boatyards are now a city park that stretches for miles down the river. Admission charged to the museum; (615) 247–3211.

The city fathers of Blountville say that there are more original log houses along their city's main street than in any other town in the state. Whether that's true or not, there are a great many vintage buildings to see here. One of those, **The Deery Inn,** played an important part in the frontier era of this part of the state. Built during the late 1700s, the building is actually three buildings: a two-story hewn-log house, a three-story cut-stone house, and a two-story frame structure, all built adjacent to one another and joined together. It's now a private residence, but the architecture can still be appreciated from the sidewalk.

Across the street is the **Cannonball House Antiques and Gifts** shop. This old structure got its name from a big cannonball hole that still exists in the building.

A walking-tour map of Blountville is available, and most of the buildings are decorated and open to the public around Christmas.

Continue on Highway 37 out of Blountville and head south to Bluff City. Just as you cross the Boone Lake bridge coming into town, look to your left and you'll see this community's answer to what to do with old railroad abutments. The trestle has been removed and a mural painted on the stone wall. The colorful painting depicts a train coming out of a tunnel. It's a nice touch.

For the best barbecue meal in eastern Tennessee, continue through Bluff City and head out Old Highway 19E (not the new four-lane Highway 19E). There you'll find the ↄ**Ridgewood Restaurant.** Grace Proffitt and her restaurant are legendary in these parts. She has been dishing up barbecued pork and beef since 1948, and most barbecue experts from coast to coast agree that hers is some of the best in the country.

Much of the cooking is done out front where patrons can watch. Although many other items take up space on the menu, it's the barbecue that brings people through the doors. She makes about sixteen gallons of her special sweet-and-sour sauce a day. "It's a secret recipe, and I keep it in my head," she claims. Her son Terry, who works the eatery with her, is the only other person who knows the exact blends.

Coleslaw is put on all barbecue sandwiches, and various other hot sauces accompany hers to the table. Great northern white beans are prepared in her sauce and served along with hand-cut french fries on the popular platters. No reservations are taken, and the weekends tend to get crowded. Open every day but Monday; (615) 538–7543.

4

Perhaps one of the most historically significant extant structures in the state is **Rocky Mount,** a two-story log cabin in Piney Flats. Built in 1770, Rocky Mount is the oldest original territorial capital in the United States and one of the oldest buildings in the state.

It was the capital of "The Territory of the United States south of the river Ohio" from 1790 until a new capitol was built in Knoxville. With two stories and nine rooms, pine paneling, and real glass windows, the structure was a mansion by frontier standards, and it quickly became a gathering place for people across the entire frontier.

Today the house is open to the public daily, as is the adjoining **Overmountain Museum,** which shows the early life of the area. First-person interpretation provides visitors with a true sense of what was taking place in 1791. Guides talk with you as they would have in that year and stay in character for your entire visit. On Route 11E; (615) 538–7396.

Johnson County

This county is surrounded by the hills of the Appalachian Mountains, and the businesses and attractions reflect that way of life quite nicely. Throughout the county you'll see small handwritten signs hanging from mailboxes advertising handmade quilts or birdhouses for sale. Farther down any road, you'll pass through a crossroads community with a small general store stocked with local Appalachian crafts.

In Mountain City, about the only thing you won't find are crowds. Within a few-block area of the downtown section, you'll find numerous antique and gift shops selling a whole variety of neat things.

North of Mountain City, on Highway 91, is Laurel Bloomery, a small community of about seventy people. There, ⊃**Iron Mountain Stoneware** makes its world-famous line, which can be found in posh department stores across the country. More than 600 stores sell the products created here at the foot of Iron Mountain.

Iron Mountain is one of the few firms in the country that still produces high-fired stoneware dinnerware. Most of the work is

done by hand, but the owner says that just enough mechaniza-
tion is used to keep the process efficient. "We do everything here
but mine the clay," said one employee. The pottery operates an
on-site retail store that carries a full line of the twenty-four separate patterns they create.

The tours are informal and are given on request; (615)
727–8888.

South of Mountain City on Highway 421 is ⊃**Trade,** the oldest
unincorporated community in the state. It's the spot where, in
1673, the first English-speaking white man set foot on Tennessee
soil. Situated on an old buffalo trail, the community flourished as
a resting place for those traveling the three major paths through
the wilderness that crossed at this point.

By the 1790s, the area had a country store, a post office, a
blacksmith shop, and a handful of cabins, and today it's about as
low-key as it was then—no big signs and no souvenir shops.
"Trade Days" is held each June, when the entire county comes
out to celebrate the heritage of the area.

In Trade, at the intersection of Route 421 and Highway 67,
Jack Belk has his **Casa Que Pasa antique shop,** and it's exactly
what you'd expect out here in the mountains. He specializes in
vintage quilts, stained-glass windows, antique furniture, primi-
tives, and art deco. Jack's partner, Maggie Houlihans, specializes
in Victorian florals and vintage clothing. Located in the old Trade
School, they are open every weekend, or weekdays by chance or
appointment; (615) 727–9172.

Carter County

One of the state's remaining original covered bridges crosses
the Doe River in downtown Elizabethton and is the focal point
for the city's riverside park. Built in 1882, ⊃**The Kissing Bridge**
(as the locals call it) is the oldest such structure in the state.

For many years, a tall Frazier fir tree on Elk Street near downtown Elizabethton was considered the tallest such tree in the
world. Then the gloomy day came when officials found it was
only the second tallest. But since the tallest is never decorated at
Christmas, they now decorate the fir in Elizabethton, making it
the tallest *decorated* Frazier fir tree in the world.

Flying missionaries to and from remote parts of the world is quite difficult and requires pilots trained in a "seat of your pants" style of piloting. In Elizabethton, **Moody Missionary Aviation** trains pilots to do just that. A division of Chicago's Moody Bible Institute, the aviation school provides three years of technical training for a student who has already completed two years of missionary studies.

Once students graduate, they are "free agents" who can work for any missionary organization. "Our pilots are capable of flying in the worst of conditions with no instruments and, most often, no formal landing strip," said flight instructor Bruce Hendrich. "And since they are also trained missionaries, they understand the importance of their jobs."

The school also functions as a "regular" flight school and operates a charter service. In addition, it is under contract with the city of Elizabethton to run the city airport. The entire operation is open for public tours, and plane rides over the mountainous areas are available from here; (615) 543-3534.

About 20 miles southeast of Elizabethton on Highway 143 is **Roan Mountain State Park.** The park itself lies at the foot of Roan Mountain, one of the highest peaks (6,313 feet) in the Eastern United States, but that's not what makes this park so special. On the side of that mountain is one of the largest rhododendron gardens in the country. More than 600 acres of color bloom each June, making the area a striking display of pinks and purples. The park is the best place in the area to view fall foliage. A campground and cabins offer overnighters grand vistas of the mountains.

Walking and hiking trails line the mountain with numerous "scenic overlooks." The **Dave Miller Homestead,** a preserved farm, is located in a hollow atop Strawberry Mountain. The Miller family first settled in the area around 1870 and for generations lived in virtual seclusion. Today, the farm is preserved intact and serves as a model of early Appalachian life. Frank Miller, grandson of Dave, is the caretaker and is eager to share his knowledge and humor with visitors. Admission free; (615) 772-3303.

Farther down Highway 321 toward Johnson City is the **Sinking Creek Baptist Church.** The log structure, built in 1803, is the oldest Baptist church in the state and is open to the public on weekdays during the warmer months. It's located next to the new church; (615) 928-3222.

Unicoi County

The county seat community of ꓛErwin probably holds the distinction of being the only town ever to put an elephant on trial for murder, find it guilty, and carry out the death penalty.

"Murderous Mary," a circus elephant who trampled her owner to death, was hanged from a railroad derrick before 5,000 spectators in 1916. Newspaper clippings and photos of that event are but a few of the interesting items in the **Unicoi County Heritage Museum,** housed in a turn-of-the-century home on the grounds of the **National Fish Hatchery** on Highway 23.

The hatchery was established in 1894, and the ten-room superintendent's residence was constructed in 1903. By the early 1980s, the house wasn't being used by the superintendent, so the federal government signed an agreement allowing the county to use it as a museum. In addition to the story of Murderous Mary, various displays highlight local pottery production, the history of local railroading, and on the second floor is a replica of the city's turn-of-the-century Main Street.

In "Grandmother's Attic" is a display of quilts, antique dolls, and children's toys, all displayed as they might be in your own grandma's attic.

Outside, the fish hatchery is still in operation and produces about 18 million rainbow trout eggs each year. Tours are available at the hatchery as well as at the museum. Admission free; (615) 743–4712 for the hatchery, (615) 743–9449 for the museum.

Bring your lunch; the entire area is a beautiful parklike setting, complete with a picnic pavilion and rest rooms.

Washington County

The sixteen counties that now make up the eastern tip of Tennessee were at one time united together in an effort to become a state by themselves. The framework for the state of Franklin was set when about 30,000 white settlers crossed the Appalachian Mountains and founded several settlements in this area, which was a part of North Carolina at the time.

Leaders met in Jonesborough and created a bill of rights for their new state and requested the lawmakers of North Carolina to allow the new state. They refused, but Franklin, under the leadership of John Sevier, continued the battle for several years, until 1788. Several skirmishes between Franklin and North Carolina militia took place in the area.

Although never recognized as an official state, Franklin operated like a sovereign government with an assembly, administered justice, and negotiated treaties with the Indians.

Eight years after the fight for the quasi-state ended, Sevier became the first governor of the state of Tennessee, which incorporated the former boundaries of Franklin. Jonesborough, chartered in 1779, seventeen years before there was a Tennessee, holds the distinction of being the oldest incorporated area in the state. And thanks to an ambitious restoration effort, much of the city appears as it did more than a century ago.

There are more than twenty-seven points of interest on the walking-tour map of the historic downtown area, including the historic **Chester Inn,** where a young Andrew Jackson stayed while working on his law degree in 1788.

Many of the old buildings along the main streets now house a wide array of specialty shops. One particular structure, the ⊃**Old Town Hall,** at 144 East Main Street, was restored in 1982 and now houses about fifty crafts-oriented shops, plus a small deli restaurant. Down the street is "Mauk's (more than a) Pharmacy." Considered the state's oldest continuously operating drug store, the business has been in the same family since 1891.

Over behind the courthouse, at 102 Woodrow Avenue, the ⊃**Parson's Table Restaurant** is located in the circa-1870 First Christian Church building and parsonage. Owned by Debra and "Chef" Jeff Myron, the Victorian dining hall offers classical music, linen tablecloths and napkins, and about twenty entrees for dinner every night except Monday. A Sunday buffet is served and there is a daily luncheon special. This is truly an oasis of elegant dining among the barbecue restaurants of eastern Tennessee. Complete dinners range from $10 to $20. No alcohol is sold, but bring your own wine and they'll keep it chilled for you. Reservations suggested for dinner; (615) 753–8002.

Tobie Bledsoe owns several historic buildings in the downtown area and has turned two of them into the best bed-and-breakfast facilities in town. All are within walking distance of the rest of the historic district. (615) 753–9223.

The **Jonesborough History Museum,** at 117 Boone Street, is located inside the visitors center and is a good place to start your visit to this historic area. Brochures, maps, and a short film will get you started in the right direction. Make sure you pick up a free copy of "An Introduction to Building Watching," a guide on how to get the most out of viewing historic structures. It really is helpful, even if you think you already know architecture. Horse-drawn carriage tours of the area are available. Open daily; (615) 753–5961.

Greene County

Contrary to the myth started by Walt Disney, Davy Crockett was not born on a mountaintop in Tennessee; he was born along the banks of Nolichuckey River, near the mouth of Limestone Creek. Today that birth spot, just outside of the small community of Limestone, is marked by the ⊃**Davy Crockett Birthplace State Historical Area.**

Born in 1786, David (he never signed his name Davy) went on to become the "King of the Wild Frontier." His name and legend can rightfully be claimed by many areas in the state. He was born

Davy Crockett's Birthplace, Limestone

10

here in the east, he ran a gristmill in the center of the state, and he was elected to Congress from western Tennessee.

But here is where it all began. A reproduction of his birthplace cabin has been constructed, with the cornerstone of his original cabin on display. Probably the most unusual aspect of this park is the monument erected in the late 1960s by a local civic organization. In honor of Crockett's stature as a national hero, each of the fifty states is represented in the wall of the monument. Stones native to each state are incorporated in the wall and engraved with the respective state's name.

The park, located off U.S. Highway 11E, has a campground, swimming pool, picnic facilities, and a visitors center. Open year-round; cabin open daily during the warmer months; (615) 257–2167.

Within walking distance of the park is the **Snapp Inn Bed and Breakfast.** Owned by Dan and Ruth Dorgan, the inn is a restored 1815 Federal brick home, chock-full of antiques. Rates are $40 single, $50 double, and include a full breakfast. Nonsmoking patrons only; (615) 257–2482.

Fifteen minutes down Highway 321 is the county seat city of Greeneville, which happens to be the only Greeneville in the United States that uses that middle *e* in its name.

It was to this city that an eighteen-year-old boy moved in 1826 to establish a tailor business for himself. Several years later, that boy, Andrew Johnson, became the country's seventeenth president. Today, Johnson's Greeneville years are highlighted at the **Andrew Johnson National Historic Site,** in the downtown section. His small tailor shop has been preserved and is inside the site's visitors center. Across the street is the brick home in which he lived from 1831–1851, and on Main Street is another house he lived in from 1851–1875, while he was president. The cemetery where he and his family are buried is a few miles away. All four attractions are open every day except Christmas Day. The visitors center is located at the corner of College and Depot streets; (615) 638–3551.

Across College Street from the Johnson site is the **Ye Olde Tourist Trappe** crafts cooperative. Managed by Sue Hice, the shop features works from more than 150 local craftspeople and includes everything from quilts to wooden toys to wreaths to cookbooks of local delicacies. Open daily; (615) 639–1567.

A walking-tour map of Greeneville is available that highlights thirty-six historic areas or structures of the community, including **St. James Episcopal Church,** circa 1850. Its interior is exceptional, with walnut woodwork and pews, a slave gallery, and the oldest working organ in the state. (615) 638–4111.

Greeneville's ↄ**Tusculum College,** founded in 1794, is the oldest college south of the Ohio River and west of the Allegheny Mountains. It was the twenty-eighth college founded in America, is the oldest college in the state, and is the oldest coed college associated with the Presbyterian Church.

Eight buildings on the campus were constructed between 1841 and 1928 and comprise the college's historic district. A walking tour of the campus is included in the city's walking-tour brochure.

The college's **Andrew Johnson Library and Museum** is the state's largest presidential library and houses a great many of the president's books, papers, and manuscripts, as well as those of his family. In addition, the library houses almost 200 original Civil War–era newspapers from throughout the country. (615) 638–1111.

Five miles southeast of town on Highway 70 the **University of Tennessee** has an experimental farm that specializes in research on burly tobacco. The farm, according to Phil Hunter, its superintendent, concentrates on developing disease-resistant varieties and on labor-saving production practices. The fall is the best time to visit the farm. That's when the cutting, handling, and drying procedures are undertaken, but Hunter assures us that if you're not familiar with tobacco production, a trip to the farm anytime would be quite fascinating. Tobacco is the leading cash crop of Tennessee, which is the third largest tobacco producer in the country. (615) 638–6532.

Hawkins County

The ↄ**Tennessee Mountaineer Restaurant,** on Highway 11W in Church Hill, specializes in Hillbilly Fried Chicken. "It's not the way we fix them that's so special," said owner Clarence Painter. "It's the chickens themselves. They have one leg shorter than the other so they can walk on the side of the mountains around here."

Whether you believe that or not, you can believe that only good food is served up in this family restaurant. One indication that the food and environment are good is that this eatery is the meeting spot for five civic organizations and two hunting groups.

Make sure you leave room for dessert. Clarence's kitchen turns out peach cobbler, hot fudge cake, and chocolate pie. As a side dish, ask for the fried apples; they are prepared in a great-tasting blend of maple syrup and brown sugar. Open daily at 6:00 A.M.; (615) 357–5511. Before you leave, pick up a free copy of the mountain-talk primer that Clarence keeps near the cash register. Read and memorize it, and you'll be able to communicate with the mountain folk during the rest of your journey across Tennessee.

In downtown Rogersville, the ꓛ**Hale Springs Inn** is considered to be the oldest continuously operating inn in the state. Built in 1824, the inn has been totally restored and today offers a dining room and eight guest rooms, all with fireplaces. Much of the original 1824 structure is evident, including the staircases and the wooden floors throughout. Each room is furnished with antique furniture. All three Tennessee presidents, Johnson, Jackson, and Polk, stayed here, and all have guest rooms named after them. Room rates range from $40 to $65, which includes breakfast. (615) 272–5171.

Down the street from the inn is the **1890 railroad depot.** Located on Depot Street, at the railroad, the structure was renovated in 1989 and now holds the county history museum, the chamber of commerce, and the visitors center. (615) 272–2186.

Most of the old structures in downtown Rogersville have been restored, and the entire district is on the National Register of Historic Places. A walking tour of the historic district includes the Hawkins County Courthouse. Built in 1836, the building is the oldest original courthouse still in use in the state.

Most of the Main Street retail businesses now sell antiques or crafts, but there are still a few old-time offices and clothing stores along the way.

Hancock County

Scott Collins works at the courthouse in Sneedville, and he's considered to be a member of the nation's smallest minority. He's a Melungeon, and there are not too many true Melungeons left.

For years there had been various theories of where the Melungeons came from, but Collins said no one was able to prove any of them true or false. Then, in mid-1992, an Atlanta researcher, himself part Melungeon, was able to trace the race back to A.D. 710 to Southern Spain and Portugal. In a nutshell, Melungeons are descendants of the Phoenicians and the Carthaginians, the conquerors of both of those countries.

Through a series of events, they were forced to leave their homelands, and a group of several hundred was put ashore off the coast of South Carolina sometime between 1530 and 1614. Known then as Moriscos, members of the group made their way inland and eventually settled in the mountains of western North Carolina and east Tennessee. During their heyday, the center of their life in this county was high atop Newman's Ridge.

Characteristically, Melungeons had smooth olive-colored skin, straight black hair, dark eyes, and high cheek bones. The women were shorter than average, and the men were tall and straight.

Because of mixed marriages during the 200 years or so the Melungeons called this area home, there are no "true" members of the race. "There are no distinctive traits evident in us today that make us look any different than anyone else," Collins said.

Up on Newman's Ridge today, you'll find a few old, grown-over buildings, and a cemetery. There are no good roads to get there, and most of the year it takes a four-wheel-drive vehicle to do so.

Collins is kind of the unofficial historian of the race as well as the area, and his office wall is covered with photos dating back to before 1900. Researching his race is almost impossible, since the county courthouse burned down twice during the years, destroying all records. Call Collins at the courthouse when you're in town, and he'll be glad to invite you over to see the photos and to talk about the Melungeons. (615) 733-4524.

You have to be going to Sneedville to get there. No major highways lead there, and there are only three state highways in the entire county. In a way, the area is a part of the state that time has forgot. There aren't too many pre-1900 structures in the county, and most of Sneedville proper reminds you of the 1950s.

In mid-1989, the county received its first national food franchise, a Hardees restaurant. All other businesses are local, family-owned establishments. Total county population is about 7,000.

Off the Beaten Path in the Mountainous East

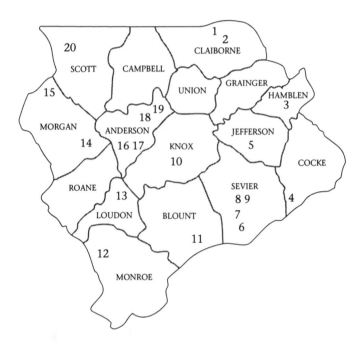

1. World's Largest Stalagmite
2. Lincoln Memorial University
3. The Murrell Flyer
4. Moonshine Capital of the World
5. Davy Crockett's Marriage License
6. LeConte Lodge
7. Hillbilly Golf Course
8. Dollywood
9. Giant Cuckoo Clock
10. Sunsphere
11. Little River Railroad and Lumber Company
12. The Lost Sea
13. Crosseyed Cricket
14. America's Smallest Library
15. Rugby's Utopian Community
16. "Secret City"
17. American Museum of Science and Energy
18. Museum of Appalachia
19. Lenoir Family Museum
20. Big South Fork National River and Recreation Area

The Mountainous East

Claiborne County

The quaint little village of Cumberland Gap rests just a few miles from one of the most historic natural passageways of all time. Much of the westward movement of early America came through this V-shaped indentation in the Appalachian Mountain chain, a wall of rock that stretches from Maine to Georgia.

It was 1775 when Daniel Boone and his thirty axmen hacked out the Wilderness Road through the gap to open up the "western frontier" and the fertile farmlands on the other side. It was the first road platted by a white man in the state. That byway became a major thoroughfare and is now a four-lane highway.

At the top of the gap, a marker in the **Cumberland Gap National Historic Park** shows where the states of Kentucky, Virginia, and Tennessee meet. It is said that from the top, those three states, plus Georgia and North Carolina, can be seen on a clear day. A visitors center and museum are part of the park. (606) 248–2817.

Directly below that point, deep beneath the mountain, the ⊃**World's Largest Stalagmite** can be found in Cudjo's Caverns. It's 65 feet high, 35 feet in circumference, and still growing. Officials say the formation, which they call the "Pillar of Hercules," is approximately eighty-five million years old. Admission charged; (703) 861–2203.

The village of Cumberland Gap was founded by English settlers and today shows a strong English influence in its architecture. The downtown section has been virtually untouched by modernization for fifty years. The opening scene of a movie was filmed here in 1988, and according to one of the downtown businessmen, only one sign had to be removed to make the town look like a small town of the 1930s.

A few miles south on Highway 25E is Harrogate, the home of ⊃**Lincoln Memorial University.** Founded in 1896 as a living memorial to President Lincoln, the school's charter mandated the establishment of a museum to house memorabilia of the Lincoln era. Today, the Lincoln Library and Museum on the campus houses the third largest collection of Lincolniana and Civil War items in the world.

16

One of the most historic items in the museum is the ebony cane the president was carrying on the night he was assassinated. The school itself is beautiful and is a nice tribute to mountain life in east Tennessee. Take time to walk through the campus. Admission charged to museum; (615) 869–3611.

Farther south on Highway 25E near Tazewell is the **Springdale Old Log Church.** Built in 1795, a year before Tennessee became a state, the church is still the site of Baptist services one Sunday a month. (615) 626–4149.

Grainger County

When Andrew Johnson came to Tennessee to establish a tailor shop, he spent a few months in Rutledge before relocating to nearby Greeneville. A reproduction of Johnson's first shop has been built and is located in front of Grainger County Courthouse, on the original site.

A few blocks away is the circa-1848 Grainger County Jail, the oldest standing brick jailhouse in Tennessee. Restored by the county's historical society, the facility now houses the society and serves as a public meeting house for the area's clubs and organizations. Inside, the original metal stairs and wall partitions are intact. Although not open on a regular basis, Frances Hickle will be glad to show you around and tell you about the hanging just outside the front door. (615) 828–3688.

Near Washburn, Ann Stover Hurst has a cottage industry called the **Shenanndoah Farm.** There, she makes brooms and mops entirely by hand in the old Appalachian style, with natural vine and root handles. No machinery is used at all, making each creation unique. She also grows and packages herbs and produces pencil sketches of early mountain life. (615) 497–2608.

Hamblen County

In the 1790s, Davy Crockett's dad opened a small, six-room tavern near present-day Morristown. That's where little Davy spent his early years. In the 1950s a reproduction of that tavern was built on the original site, and today the **David Crockett Tavern and Museum** serves as a frontier museum honoring the Crockett family and other early Tennessee pioneers. The tavern is full of period utensils and furnishings. It's located at 2002 East Morningside Drive. Open daily, May through October; (615) 587–9900.

The first patented flying machine in America was developed by Melville Murrell, a Morristown preacher. Patented in 1877, a good while before the Wright brothers, the ↻**Murrell Flyer** flew several hundred yards under bicycle-type power. Parts of the original flyer, including its wings and some of the frame, are on display at the city's Rose Center. A video presentation features interviews with some of Murrell's descendants and several photos of the plane itself.

Built in 1892 and saved from destruction in 1975 by a community action group, the **Rose Center** was the area's first school. It now serves as a community cultural center and includes a history museum, art gallery, exhibit space, and gift shop. (615) 581–4330.

Each October, the **Mountain Makin's Festival** is held on the grounds of the Rose Center and features one of east Tennessee's finest juried crafts shows. Two music stages feature various forms of local mountain music and other activities. (615) 586–6382.

Cocke County

Cosby was settled in 1783 by a corn farmer searching for a quiet, peaceful life. Corn remained the main crop for many years, and it didn't take long before the discovery was made that it was easier to transport it in the liquid form known as moonshine. For many years, the area was known as the ↻**"Moonshine Capital of the World."**

Today, the unincorporated "downtown" of Cosby consists of a post office, bar, bank, a small grocery store, and a gas station. In the hollow bordering the Great Smoky Mountains National Park, the area is still peaceful and quiet. The **Schilling Family Folk Life Center,** about a mile from the post office on Highway 32, is advertised as the "kind of shop you hope to find when you visit the Smokies." The family makes and plays dulcimers, but the store also sells crafts and products from more than 100 local craftspeople. (615) 487–5543.

Apples are now considered one of the area's biggest cash crops, and there are five or six major orchards that sell directly from their farms. Also, many smaller orchards have been planted and produce excellent crops. Look for "Apples For Sale" signs along the roads. One of the area's oldest orchards is owned and operated by the third generation of Baxters, out Highway 73 from Cosby; they sell cider and a home blend of honey that can't be beat.

The *ramp* is an onionlike vegetable native to the foothills of the southern Appalachian Mountains. The odd-looking plant has been described as the "vilest-smelling, sweetest-tasting vegetable in the world." Early settlers attributed special medicinal qualities to the ramp.

Raw, parboiled, fried, or scrambled in eggs, it was regarded as a necessary spring tonic to ward off the sluggishness of winter. In the 1950s Cosby introduced the ramp to the rest of the world when it established its first annual spring festival in the plant's honor. Each spring, thousands come here to enjoy activities and truckloads of ramps.

Frederich and Maria Marx, owners of **Fort Marx,** sold their restaurant and moved out into the country to retire. But the fans of their old establishment followed them, and it wasn't long before the Marxes were dishing up some of their fine German food and serving "friends" out of their double-wide mobile home.

The crowds grew, and Frederich kept building onto the trailer. Today, Fort Marx serves the best German food in this part of the state. "We are known around the world," Frederich is quick to point out. "We've had people in here from every major country in the world, and I can prove it." He dusts off a series of guest books and starts pointing out the various visitors, along with stories on each one.

The menu, hand printed and stapled onto the wall, has an additional sign hanging from the bottom: "Maria can cook any-thing that walks, crawls, flies, or swims. But no oysters or clams, please. If it ain't on the menu, ask fer it."

The small funky restaurant can seat forty-five patrons. "And that has actually happened a time or two," Frederich adds. They've been here for twelve years, halfway up a hill above the Little Pigeon River. No road signs, only their name on the mailbox, a few miles off Wilton Springs Road, near Exit 440 off Interstate 40. Open at 5:00 P.M., Monday through Saturday; (615) 487–2112.

In the county seat city of Newport, the **Cocke County Museum** is located upstairs in the Community Center building. Downstairs are the chamber of commerce and tourist information offices. This is a good place to start a tour of the county.

Jefferson County

Dandridge, the second oldest city in the state, is also the only city in the United States named for Martha Dandridge Washington, wife of our first president. The Jefferson County Museum, located on the first level of the circa-1845 county courthouse, has a good collection of regional history, including ⊃**Davy Crockett's Marriage License.** Admission free; open during courthouse hours; (615) 397–3800.

Information on the walking tour of downtown Dandridge, which features more than thirty structures on the National Historic Register, is available from the courthouse as well as from many stores throughout the area.

The **Glenmore Mansion** is considered by many architects as an almost perfect example of Victorian architecture. Built in 1869, the twenty-seven-room, five-story mansion is fully furnished with antiques of the period. In eastern Tennessee, where most historical preservation efforts are saved for pre-1850 architecture, it's good to see the preservation of the Victorian era. Located at 1280 N. Chucky Pike in Jefferson City; open Thursday through Sunday afternoons from 1:00 to 5:00 P.M., May through October; (615) 475–7643.

In the southwestern part of the county on Highway 411, **Chestnut Hill** was begun as a company town. A. J. Bush was a schoolteacher and a general-store owner when he created a business to help provide the local men a chance for employment. A. J. Bush & Co. was founded in 1907 as a tomato processing plant. Today, there are eight plants processing canned vegetables that serve about 75 percent of the country.

Remnants of early Chestnut Hill are still evident. The company store at the gates of the plant is still there and sells "just about everything." During the 1920s and 1930s, the Bush family paid its employees partially in cash and partially in scrip, redeemable for merchandise and food at the company's general store.

J. C. Thornton, who started with the company during the war

when he was fourteen, is considered the unofficial historian of the company and the town and is willing to share his stories with anyone who is interested. Public tours of the plant are not allowed because of insurance regulations, but J. C. has plenty of photos. Call first; (615) 623–2361.

Sevier County

As the most visited national park in the country with ten million visitors a year, the **Great Smoky Mountains National Park** is hardly off the beaten path. But the facility is so large at 500,000 acres and has so many nooks and crannies that it isn't difficult to get away from the madding crowds.

There are established camping areas throughout the park, but camping is also permitted in the undeveloped regions as well. Special backcountry permits are needed for that.

The Sugarland's Visitors Center is located 2 miles inside the park from Gatlinburg and has maps and other information about the entire park, as well as exhibits on what one will most likely see during a visit.

Featuring more species of plants than any other area on our continent, this official International Biosphere Reserve is a true gem in Tennessee travel opportunities.

Within the boundaries, there are sixteen peaks towering above 6,000 feet, including Clingman's Dome, which, at 6,643 feet, is the highest point in Tennessee.

One of the park's most unusual attractions is ↄ**LeConte Lodge,** a great place to stay while in the mountains if you enjoy walking. In fact, that's the only way you can get there, and it's not the easiest walk you'll ever make. The lodge rests on top of the third highest peak in the park, making it the highest guest lodge in the eastern United States. The shortest (and steepest) hike to the lodge is $5^{1}/_{2}$ miles long, which is about a four-hour hike for a person in good condition. Once there, you'll find no electricity, phones, or showers—just a great view and wonderful food; (615) 429–5704.

Cades Cove was a thriving mountain community in the 1850s, with about 685 residents and 15,000 acres of usable farmland under cultivation. Today the area is as it was then, with original buildings in original locations, so the visitor can get a

21

Cades Cove Grist Mill
Great Smoky Mountains National Park

true sense of the spaciousness of early mountain life. An 11-mile self-guided auto loop tour gives the best idea of the culture of the region. Most homes, churches, and stores are open to the public and are accessible by dirt paths.

It's easy to get to the scenic panoramas in the park; there are plenty of designated pull-offs and observation areas. The Foothill Parkway provides some of the best sight-seeing from your auto, and possibly the best view in the park comes after a short walk through the wilderness to the observation tower at Clingman's Dome.

Outside the park at 3889 Wonderland Way, you'll find the rustic **Wonderland Hotel,** which features a front porch lined with old-fashioned rockers. A sign at the door proudly reads: "We have no radio, no TV, and no telephone in every room."

The tourist destination city of Gatlinburg is located near the main entrance to the park and is considered its main gateway. Souvenir and craft shops and various attractions line the main streets, while honeymoon houses and motels line the back streets.

Among the attractions, there are a few gems: If you happen to be one of the growing corps of people who love the macabre, a trip to the **Seven Gables Haunted House** is a must. It's on the Parkway (main strip), a block from **Ripley's Believe It or Not,** up from the **Guinness World Records Exhibition Center,** down from the **Mystery Mansion,** and under the **Space Needle.**

Since parking is at such a premium in Gatlinburg, perhaps the best deal in town is the 25-cent ride on its rapid transit system, the trolley. During peak season, the entire city can become one large parking lot, so find a place to park on the edge of town or at your hotel and rely on the trolley.

The ↻**Hillbilly Golf Course** may well be one of the most unusual miniature golf courses in the world. To get to the first hole, you must ride an incline up to a point 300 feet above the city. Two 18-hole courses, with all sorts of mountaineer hazards, including a genuine outhouse and a moonshine still, are carved out of the mountainside. Near Traffic Light Number 2; (615) 436–7470.

America's first **Motion Master Movie Theater** opened for business in late 1989 and is the most high-tech family attraction the city has to offer. A wide screen, individual computer-controlled seat movement, and "surround sound" all help create a you-are-there sensation. Theatergoers experience the jolts, bumps, and hairpin turns of adventures such as monster roller coasters and dune buggy races. Located at Traffic Light Number 8; (615) 436–9763.

Head north on Route 441 out of Gatlinburg, go through a part of the national forest, and 5 miles later, you'll be in Pigeon Forge, where a 25-cent trolley ride, with fifty stops, helps you avoid traffic congestion. Similar to Gatlinburg in its attractions, this city's main draw is country singer Dolly Parton's theme park, ↻**Dollywood.** Country music prevails in the park, as do country crafts and good country cooking. It's easy to find: Turn east at the big Dollywood billboard at the corner of Dollywood Lane. The park's welcome center is located under the sign.

The **Dixie Stampede** has an interesting concept for a southern dinner theater. While eating a southern feast, patrons watch a live show in the central dirt-covered arena. The Western Show features thirty horses, Conestoga wagons, pig racing, bull riding, steer wrestling, and a bunch more good-old-boy activities. For added flavor, the Northerners sit on one side, the Southerners on the other. Reservations are sometimes necessary; (615) 453–4400.

Along the Parkway, across the road from the red-roofed Factory Merchants Mall, you can pan for your own treasures at **The Mine.** Rubies, sapphires, and other precious stones are mixed with the dirt, and it's finders keepers. A gem shop is next door for those who want their finds mounted in earrings or rings. (615) 453–7712.

At the Bavarian Haus in Bell Tower Square, located next to the Pigeon Forge Welcome Center, a ↄ**Giant Cuckoo Clock,** billed as the world's largest, goes into action every fifteen minutes. Five-foot-tall wooden musicians play while a 3-foot-tall cuckoo bird

Giant Cuckoo Clock, Pigeon Forge

makes its presence known. Inside the clock a shop sells clocks, Hummels, and other old-world gifts. (615) 453–0414.

At **Carbo's Police Museum,** along the Parkway, you'll see the 1974 Corvette in which Tennessee's *Walking Tall* sheriff, Buford Pusser, was killed. (For more on Buford Pusser, see the McNairy County entries in The Western Plains chapter.) Also at Carbo's are displays featuring police badges, uniforms, weapons, and other police items from around the world.

Applewood Farms is located just off Route 441 at 230 Lonesome Valley Road, right where Pigeon Forge and Sevierville meet. A working apple orchard, the barn was converted into a cider mill in 1981, just in time to attract people from forty-five different states and ten foreign countries who were in the area visiting the 1982 World's Fair in nearby Knoxville. Owners Bill Kilpatrick and Bon Hicks knew they had something going and started to expand.

Today, in addition to the cider mill, they have a bakery, an apple butter kitchen, a fudge kitchen, a candy factory, a smokehouse, and a gift shop featuring crafts, gifts, and souvenir items. In 1987 their old farmhouse home was turned into the Applewood Farmhouse Restaurant. On the menu you'll find traditional items such as prime rib and steaks, but you'll also find local favorites, including fried biscuits and fresh Smoky Mountain trout. One of the favorites is trout cake, made from crumbled trout mixed with cheese and onions. But save room for some wonderful apple dessert. The homemade apple pies are always a favorite, but the apple fritters, accompanied by homemade apple butter, are also high on the list for apple lovers. Located across the road from the Little Pigeon River, there are plenty of huge shade trees to sit under while you wait your turn. Open daily for breakfast, lunch, and dinner. Special meals and hours for Thanksgiving and Christmas; (615) 453–9319.

About 4 miles north on Route 441, or the Dolly Parton Parkway as they call it around here, is the downtown section of Dolly's hometown, Sevierville. Stop and ask about her and you'll be amazed at how many "good friends" this lady has. Less commercial than the other communities along Route 441, the downtown section has retained most of its small, mountain atmosphere. In a walking tour of twenty-six historic landmarks, you'll get to see a bronze, life-size statue of Dolly.

Knox County

Heading to Knoxville from Sevierville on Highway 441/411, you'll pass an abundance of antique and craft shops, potteries, and souvenir and gift shops. When the highways split, continue on Highway 441 into Knoxville until you cross the Tennessee River. That big golden ball you see high in the air to your left as you cross the river is the ↄ**Sunsphere,** the 300-foot-tall centerpiece of the 1982 World's Fair.

The Knoxville Convention and Visitors Bureau now calls it home, but for a small fee, visitors can ride to the top and survey the fair site and the downtown section of the city. The adjacent amphitheater and parklike settings are used several times during the year for festivals, concerts, and all sorts of arts-related activities. (615) 523–2316.

Adjacent to the fair site is an area known as the **11th Avenue Artists' Colony.** All four floors of the restored 1910 Candy Factory building and a row of Victorian houses behind it house various galleries and art workshops. Products available to the public to purchase range from ceramic mugs to textile hangings. Next to the factory building, in its new $10-million home, the **Knoxville Museum of Art** is open six days a week and offers music, lectures, and twelve exhibitions annually; (615) 525–6101.

Down the hill from the World's Fair site is the main campus of the **University of Tennessee,** where the Volunteers play their football games in the 95,000-plus-seat Neyland Stadium. It's only natural that tailgate partyers would adapt to the unique position of the stadium next to the Tennessee River. The Volunteer Navy, as it is called, starts gathering as early as Thursday before a Saturday game, and by game time as many as 300 boats have tied up. The only traffic these folks have to contend with is walking across the street to the stadium. Washington State is the only other major college stadium in the nation accessible by water.

Colorful "Big Orange" football is king in the fall, but the pinks and whites of flowering dogwood dominate the city's attention each spring. City officials estimate that about a million such trees bloom in their city each year. A Dogwood Arts Festival is held annually during late April with arts, crafts, and other activities. There are six designated "dogwood trails" in the city for self-guided tours. Free bus tours leave from the festival grounds at Market Square Mall.

East of Knoxville on Campbell Station Road, just off exit 373 of Interstate 40, among the commercial clutter of a typical suburban area, rests an oasis of country style. The **Appalachian Log Square** is a showcase for the Appalachian Log Homes company, but it is also a unique shopping area. Containing upscale country shops, a few offices, and the Apple Cake Tea Room restaurant, the complex not only shows off the workmanship of the log home company but also brings in money and provides a peaceful setting for a few shopkeepers. The tea room is a very country-oriented eatery that specializes in soups, sandwiches, and quiches. Open for lunch only, 11:00 A.M. to 2:30 P.M. Monday–Saturday. (615) 966–7848.

Blount County

Another example of the old-time company town is found along Highway 129, south of Knoxville. Incorporated in 1919, the city of Alcoa was created by the Aluminum Company of America (ALCOA). Corporate offices are in Pittsburgh, but the southern plant opened in 1913 in a town called North Maryville. Six years later, with the financial help of the corporation, the city was created and its name changed.

Sam Houston, Davy Crockett's good friend and commander at the Alamo, came to Blount County with his family when he was fourteen years of age and soon developed a fascination for the life-style of the neighboring Cherokee Indians. Soon he was adopted by the Cherokees, who called him "The Raven."

He left the Indians to take a teaching position in a one-room schoolhouse near Maryville. He had little formal education but had read every book he could get his hands on, had won every spelling contest he entered, and could recite large portions of Homer's *Iliad* from memory. His teaching career lasted one term. In March 1813, he gave up teaching to enlist in General Andrew Jackson's army to fight the Creek Indian War.

The schoolhouse where he taught still stands and is considered the oldest original schoolhouse in the state and the only building left having a close association with this famous soldier and statesman. Built in 1794, the school now houses many of Houston's artifacts, including a pair of lead knuckles with his name carved in the soft metal. Did he use them to keep order in the classroom? the guide speculates.

The site also includes a visitors center and museum exhibits. It's located 6 miles north of Maryville on Sam Houston Schoolhouse Road, off Highway 33. Open year-round; admission free; (615) 983–1550.

Before the Smoky Mountains became a national park in 1935, the little community of Townsend was a major lumbering center. The ↄ**Little River Railroad and Lumber Company,** headed by Col. W. B. Townsend, set up mills and harvested logs from the rich, fertile forests that are now federal lands.

Today, very little of that heritage exists. Townsend is a gateway to the Smokies, and tourism is the major industry. In the center of town on Highway 321, the **Smoky Junction Restaurant** specializes in all-you-can-eat catfish dinners and homemade chicken and dumplings. Out back, the **Little River Railroad and Lumber Company Museum** features a restored Shay Engine No. 2147 that was used locally during the early 1900s.

A restored train depot serves as a museum that's filled with memorabilia and photos of early railroad and lumbering industries. Usually open only on weekends. Admission free; (615) 448–6248.

The **Dogwood Mall,** on Scenic Highway 73 near the Cades Cove entrance to the park, features a variety of shops specializing in handmade mountain items, crafts, and artwork. Such items as brooms, wooden toys, quilts, stained glass, and fine art and prints are available from more than thirty local artisans.

Farther along Scenic Highway 321/73 is the **Little River Pottery & Country Store.** This is one shop that's not easy to miss or resist. On nice days, the owners line the front porch and lawn with rocking chairs and loom-woven coverlets. Inside, wheel-thrown pottery lines the walls. It's the kind of shop that beckons to you as you try to drive by.

Down the road a piece is the **Strawberry Patch Inn** where the front porch is covered with tools, toys, furniture, and other artifacts of the past.

Monroe County

Sequoyah was an uneducated, crippled Cherokee half-breed who was shunned by his peers for much of his life until, in 1821, he introduced an alphabet to his people. It was so easy to learn that soon thousands were using it. Before long the Chero-kees were more literate than most of the white men living in the area.

Sequoyah is the only man to single-handedly develop and per-fect an alphabet. In doing so, he endowed an entire nation with learning. The story of Sequoyah is told in the **Sequoyah Birth-place Museum,** located south of Vonore on Highway 360, owned and operated by the Cherokee people.

The museum is dedicated to this brilliant Native American, but it also tells a great deal about the Cherokee Indians as a nation. Displays range from Indian artifacts to a present-day Blondie comic book written in the Cherokee alphabet. An adjacent gift shop offers a wide variety of Cherokee crafts, works of art, and related books. Open daily, year-round; (615) 884–6246.

Along Highway 68, just outside of Sweetwater, you'll find something quite amazing "under the beaten path." It's ꙅ**The Lost Sea,** an attraction the Guinness Book of World Records calls the "world's largest underground lake." It's a four-and-a-half-acre "bottomless" lake, 300 feet underground.

The fifty-five-minute tour is an easy walk down to the lake. There's not a single step to concern yourself with, since all paths are sloping, with handrails. Glass-bottomed boats take you out onto the lake, and white trout will gather around the boat as you approach their end of the lake. The tour guides are local and have quite a few interesting stories to tell. They might even try to scare you a few times as you walk along. Make sure you ask about the cave's nightclub, complete with a wooden dance floor.

Lost Sea has been designated as a Registered Natural Landmark by the U.S. Department of the Interior because of the lake phe-nomenon and the abundance of rare crystalline formations throughout the cavern system. Open year-round; (615) 337–6616.

The people of the Coker Creek area are still shouting, "There's gold in them thar hills!" The community has been celebrating the **Autumn Gold Festival** each October since 1968 to high-light the area's two forms of gold—the golden color of the leaves as they turn each fall and the gold that can still be found in the creeks of the area. The festival salutes the gold-mining heritage of the region, which goes back to the late 1820s.

Harold Witt brings down a few truckloads of dirt each year from his mountain gold mine so festival-goers have a better chance of finding some real gold when they participate in one of the major events, panning for gold. There are also board splitting, syrup making, gospel and country music, and arts and crafts. The festival is held at Coker Creek Village, a family resort area a few miles out of town.

Coker Creek is located on Highway 68 a few miles from North Carolina in the Cherokee National Forest area. Downtown consists of the post office in Mamie Murphy's house. She's the postmistress and ran the postal business out of the general store until 1988 when it burned down.

Coker Creek Crafts Gallery is located one block off Highway 68 on Hot Water Road. Turn onto Hot Water across from the fire station in town. Owned by Ken and Kathleen Dalton, the business specializes in high-quality crafts and visual arts. The Daltons' baskets are known widely and are in craft collections and museums all over the country. (615) 261–2157.

Loudon County

The ꙮCrosseyed Cricket advertises that it's more than "just a place to stay." Located on Paw Paw Road a few miles from exit 364 on Interstate 40, about 20 miles southwest of Knoxville, the Cricket is a restaurant-public fishing-camping complex in a beautiful rural setting.

The restaurant is located in a 150-year-old operating gristmill and an adjacent 50-year-old log cabin overlooking the lake. The specialties are rainbow trout and channel catfish, both caught and cleaned fresh every day from the lake. Hush puppies, coleslaw, and homemade pies round out the menu.

There are two fish-out lakes, one for the trout and one for the catfish. Public fishing is allowed, and you pay by the pound for what you catch. They'll provide everything you need, including bait, for free if you didn't bring your own. If you wish, they'll clean your catch and send it over to the restaurant, where it will be cooked to your taste. Otherwise, they'll pack it in ice and you can take it home with you. There are forty-seven campsites on the far side of the lake. There's no need to have a fishing license either; they have one that covers anyone who fishes their lakes. Open year-round; closed Sundays. (615) 986–5435.

Roane County

The county is dominated by the Tennessee Valley Authority's (TVA) Watts Bar Lake. With 783 miles of lakefront, water-oriented activities are quite popular. Numerous marinas with boat rentals are scattered throughout the county. Once on the lake, island hopping is a popular activity. Hundreds of small islands make perfect secluded areas for picnicking and swimming.

Watts Bar Lake is one of several TVA lakes throughout the state that make up the chain called the "The Great Lakes of the South." Many families live on the lake in houseboats. One colony is located just west of Kingston off Highway 70.

The TVA steam plant in Kingston has free tours. There's no way you can miss it; just follow the roads to the big stacks. Elsewhere, a driving tour of the county has been developed, as has a backcountry trail driving tour. Brochures and maps for both are available from the Tourism Center, 339 West Race Street, Kingston; (615) 376–5572.

Morgan County

Dot Byrd is a celebrity in the Back Valley area, near Coalfield. She has the distinction of operating ⊃**America's Smallest Library.** She's been on the "Johnny Carson Show," and film crews from throughout the world have found the Back Valley Public Library, located in the front yard of her and husband Samuel's home. In 1989 she was the grand marshal of Coalfield High School's homecoming parade.

Every three months, the county library van pulls up and restocks the shelves. The 5-foot by 6-foot library is officially open every Tuesday from 1:00 to 5:00 P.M.

Dot has lived in the same house for the past thirty-three years and knows most of the several hundred people who live in the area that her library serves. The small building is centered in a well-kept flower garden and is never locked. "The dogs usually let us know when someone comes in," Samuel said. The library is located about 4 miles from Oliver Springs off Highway 62 on Back Valley Road. (615) 435–7819.

If it's rugged wilderness and wild white water you're looking

31

for, follow Highway 27 north to Wartburg and the **Obed Wild and Scenic River.** The area is managed by the National Park Service and the Tennessee Wildlife Resources Agency and consists of four streams within the same watershed. Through the years, they have carved their way through the landscape and have created beautiful gorges, some as deep as 500 feet.

During the rainy season, from December through April, the streams provide some of the finest, most technical white water in the nation. Some primitive camping is allowed. The visitors center for the area is located on Maiden Street, next to the Federal Building in Wartburg. (615) 346–6294.

Of the three utopian experiments in Tennessee during the late 1800s, Rugby's was the largest and has left us with the most evidence of the dreamers' struggles.

Today, seventeen of the seventy original buildings of ⊃**Rugby's Utopian Community** still stand and have been preserved or restored. A few are still inhabited by descendants of the original settlers.

In 1880, English author-reformer Thomas Hughes launched this colony with the dream that it would be "a centre in which a healthy, reverent life shall grow," At its peak in 1884, population was about 450. Today, Rugby has about seventy residents.

Hughes' vision of a utopian existence in the wilderness of Tennessee brought a taste of British culture along with it. Most of the settlers were young British of good family, and today their colorful Victorian legacies line the streets, making Rugby one of the most unusual communities in the state.

A journey through town should begin at the old Rugby Schoolhouse, which now serves as a museum and visitors center. In addition to the school, historic buildings open to visitors include the Christ Church, Episcopal, with its original hanging lamps and 1849 rosewood reed organ; Kingston Lisle, the restored home built for Hughes; and the **Thomas Hughes Free Public Library,** which still contains what is regarded as the best representative collection (7,000 volumes) of Victorian literature in America.

Two historic structures have been restored and now offer overnight accommodations with historic accuracy. The Pioneer Cottage and the Newbury House Inn are available with prior reservations. Several other early structures house gift shops and restaurants.

America's Smallest Library

If you're into ghosts and stories of haunting, you'll get your fill during your tour of Rugby's historic district. If your guide doesn't talk about the various sightings through the years, make sure you ask. Rugby is located on Route 52, a few miles west of Highway 27. Structures are open year-round (except for Thanksgiving, Christmas Eve, Christmas Day, and New Year's Day), January tours by appointment. Housing, shops, and restaurants are open year-round. (615) 628–2441.

Anderson County

In 1942, as World War II was raging, President Franklin D. Roosevelt approved the proposal by Albert Einstein to proceed in making a secret weapon. The Army Corps of Engineers chose an isolated 60,000-acre site here in Anderson County; within one year, three defense plants were built and a ⊃**"Secret City"** of 75,000 was cut out of the wilderness.

Throughout the war years, Oak Ridge, the name given the community, remained under direct supervision of the government and was surrounded by a tall barbed-wire fence. Only a handful of the workers knew the true nature of the project, and all were sworn to secrecy. It was not until the dropping of the first atomic bombs in 1945 that the inhabitants behind the fence learned that they had been members of an important team of the famed Manhattan Project. Oak Ridge produced the uranium 235 and plutonium 239, the fuel necessary for the atomic bomb.

The fences went down in 1949, and the city was incorporated. Today, most of that original "top secret" community exists. All three plants are still there, but the main emphasis in Oak Ridge now is energy research.

The original graphite reactor, which was the first full producing nuclear reactor in the world, is open to the public and is located in the X-10 (every location has a code name) building. A map of the 38-mile self-guided motor tour of the entire area is available at the visitors center, 302 S. Tulane Ave.; (615) 482–7821.

Next to the visitors center, the U.S. Department of Energy has developed one of the world's largest energy exhibitions. The ⊃**American Museum of Science and Energy** includes interactive exhibits, live demonstrations, computer displays, and filmed interpretations. All forms of energy and their relationship to humanity are explained. One favorite demonstration, especially of the young, makes a person's hair stand straight up on end. Open daily year-round, 9:00 A.M. to 5:00 P.M., closed Thanksgiving, Christmas Day, and New Year's Day. Closing extended one hour in June, July, and August. Admission free; (615) 576–3200.

The story behind the creation of the living areas of Oak Ridge is quite an amazing one. Five home designs were created and assigned to workers according to family size and job importance. Neighborhoods centered on the Town Site, which was designed to offer shopping and recreation. The high school, multifamily housing, and the hospital were also built near the Town Site. Now known as Jackson Square, a walking-tour map of that original town site is available.

West of Oak Ridge, on Highway 62, the University of Tennessee has established a forestry experiment station. The arboretum is open to the public and has three designated nature walking tours. More than 800 species of plants grow here naturally, and most of them are labeled for easy identification by visitors. Specific information about the experimental work being done at any particular time is available at the visitors center. (615) 483–3571.

The Community Crafts Center and Shop is located on Highway 61 about a mile after it crosses Interstate 75. The center was started in 1970 to "enrich the souls and pocketbooks of low-income people." Today, the nonprofit organization that runs the center works with local people to preserve traditional Appalachian crafts and techniques. All types of crafts are available. Open 9:00 A.M. to 5:00 P.M. Monday through Saturday; (615) 494–9854.

Less than a mile down the road from the crafts center is the ꓚ**Museum of Appalachia.** Founded by John Rice Irwin in 1960, the museum is considered one of the most authentic representations of early Appalachian mountain life. Dozens of cabins and buildings have been moved here and preserved in the spaciousness of their original locations. More than 250,000 items are on display. Live music and demonstrations abound as employees go about living and working in a mountain village. *Roots* author Alex Haley said he loved the museum so much that he "built a home in sight of it." He lived across the street until his death in February 1992. (615) 494–7680.

The nearby city of Norris is a great little community. Planned and built by the Tennessee Valley Authority (TVA) in 1934 as a demonstration of sound community development, the town features a green belt; a town forest, which protects the city's water supply; and houses placed in a parklike atmosphere. Now an independent municipality, Norris has preserved its original look. Brochures and information are available at the police and fire departments.

The Tennessee Valley Authority act was signed into law by President Franklin Roosevelt on May 18, 1933, and within a few weeks, the TVA's first flood-control project, the Norris Dam, was started. As the oldest TVA facility, the dam is open to visitors on occasion, although the entire operation is now run by remote control. (615) 494–0610.

The dam and the lake make up a part of the Norris Dam State Park, as does the ᴐ**Lenoir Family Museum.** Made up primarily of Will G. Lenoir's "junk" collection, items in the state-run facility date from prehistoric times to the present. The place is filled with artifacts that visitors are encouraged to pick up and touch. As the guides walk visitors through, they tell stories that bring the items to life. Many of the stories are more fun than the items themselves. To get the full benefit here, take the tour first and listen to the stories, then go back through and look at the displays at your own pace.

The museum's most treasured artifact is a European barrel organ with tiers of hand-carved wooden figures. Research shows it was made in Germany in 1826 and probably brought to America by a traveling showman. Admission free; (615) 494–9688.

Outside, the TVA has gathered two additional buildings. The **Cosby Threshing Barn,** built in the early 1800s, was one of the first threshing barns to be built in the U.S. It's full of pioneer machinery, including a wooden treadmill made in 1855. Across the field from the barn is a 1798 gristmill where corn is ground during the summer months. A gift shop is on the upper level. The entire setting is very rustic and just a short distance from the dam and a picnic area.

There are several caves within the park, but only one is open to the public. A tour of **Hill Cave,** which can be reached only by boat, is led by a park naturalist. The cave features many formations and is not equipped to handle large crowds, unlike nearby commercial caves. A few safety devices have been added, but the rest is as wild as it was when discovered. (615) 426–7461.

Campbell County

The 667-acre **Cove Lake State Recreational Area** is located on the banks of Cove Lake, near Caryville. Established in the 1930s as a recreation demonstration area by the TVA, the National Park Service, and the Civilian Conservation Corps, the lake is home to more than 400 Canada geese each winter. Surrounded by the towering Cumberland Mountains, the park is perhaps more popular with visitors in the winter than the summer. Attracted by the quiet inlets, marshes, and fields of the area, the geese come in late fall and stay through early spring. To supplement the wild food and attract geese into view, rangers put out corn near the Cove Lake Restaurant, which has a full menu of country cooking favorites and seats about 115. Open daily year-round.

The restaurant and the ranger's station and the masonry fences around them were built by the Civilian Conservation Corps.

Christmas in the Park is an annual event that county residents look forward to. The celebration features all sorts of music, lights, and decorations throughout the park. The walkways and roads are lined with candles. In the summer, the park offers an Olympic-size swimming pool open to the public. (615) 562–8355.

Scott County

This entire county has been described by many as one big natural museum. *Ruggedness* is the key word here, and one access to that ruggedness is through the ⊃**Big South Fork National River and Recreation Area.**

Authorized by Congress in 1974, the park has been frequented mainly by those who have been willing to explore the wilderness on its own terms. During the last few years, more roads, overlooks, and river access sites have been built, opening up the 100,000-acre park to less adventurous visitors.

The Big South Fork River cuts a course through one of the most spectacular chasms east of the Mississippi. The gorge is rimmed by towering bluffs of weathered sandstone, rising as high as 500 feet. It's considered to be one of the best white-water rivers in the East. In all, there are more than 80 miles of prime canoeing waters within the park.

Camping is permitted just about anywhere in the park, and mountain bikes and four-wheeled off-road vehicles are permitted on designated trails and roads. There are three developed campgrounds and the Charit Creek Hotel, dormitory style housing with bunk beds. There is no electricity here and no vehicular traffic is allowed. (615) 429–5704.

The most comfortable way to see the rugged terrain and the river is aboard the **Big South Fork Scenic Railway.** The three-hour narrated trip leaves from the historic coal-mining town of Sterns, Kentucky. The 11-mile trip takes you down gently to the bottom of the gorge, through a massive tunnel, and along high rock ledges. It then hugs the banks of the river, where you might catch a glimpse of white-water aficionados. (800) 462–5664.

Off the Beaten Path along the Plateaus and Valleys

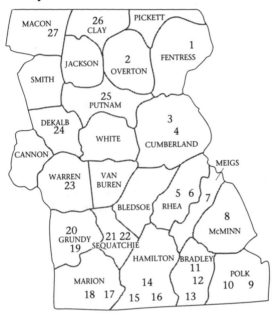

1. Alvin York State Historic Area
2. Court Square Emporium
3. Talavera De La Reina
4. Homesteads
5. Rhea County Courthouse
6. Washington Ferry
7. Spit and Whittle Gang
8. McMinn County Living Heritage Museum
9. Tennessee's Badlands
10. Ocoee Flume
11. Cherokee National Forest
12. Primitive Settlement
13. Red Clay
14. Tennessee Aquarium
15. Last Battle of the Revolution
16. Chattanooga Choo Choo
17. TVA's Raccoon Mountain Pumped Storage Facility
18. Riverside Catfish House
19. Dutch Maid Bakery
20. Old Wood Village
21. Rivendell Farm
22. Coke Ovens Historic Site
23. Cumberland Caverns
24. H & H Pig Farm
25. Cookeville Depot Museum
26. OshKosh B'Gosh
27. Red Boiling Springs

Plateaus & Valleys

Fentress County

In a valley surrounded by the Cumberland Mountains a few miles from the Kentucky border, Sergeant Alvin York, one of America's most celebrated military heroes, was born and reared. Except for the two years he spent in the war, Sergeant York spent his entire life in these mountains. But those two years put York in the history books and this part of the state on the map. Today, the ⊃**Alvin York State Historic Area** commemorates his life and career.

York's one-man firefight with the German Army in France's Argonne Forest on October 8, 1918, is now legendary. As a patrol leader, he killed twenty-five German soldiers and almost single-handedly captured another 132. As a result, he received more than forty Allied decorations and worldwide publicity.

His modest upbringing here in the Tennessee mountains and his refusal to cash in on his popularity by selling out to the media won the hearts of millions, and he returned to the valley as a bona fide hero.

York died in 1964, and four years later the state bought a large portion of land that included his family farm and the mill that he once operated. The exhibits are fine, but the real reason to visit this area is the park ranger, York's son, Andy York. He'll be more than glad to spend some time with you and tell you all sorts of stories about his famous father and the family's ties to the area. It's not too often that you get to meet a genuine hero's son whose business it is to talk about his father's life. It's a unique opportunity to put history into perspective.

The area is about 7 miles north of Jamestown on Highway 127; open daily; (615) 879–4026 and 879–5366.

A few miles south on Highway 127, at 702 Main Street North in Jamestown, the **Mountaineer Craft Center** offers the best crafts, antiques, and collectibles that this part of the state has to offer. Run by the county arts association, the crafts of more than 200 craftspersons are on display, plus there are demonstrations and classes.

The building in which the center is located is on the Historic Register and was once the dormitory of the York Institute, which is still in operation, adjacent to the center. Open March through December, Monday through Saturday, 10:00 A.M. to 5:00 P.M., and some Sundays during the peak summer months. (615) 879–4603.

Three miles south of Jamestown on Highway 127 is the **Highland Manor Winery,** which has the distinction of being the oldest winery in the state and the first American winery to be awarded the International Gold Medal for Quality in Madrid, Spain. Currently, this is one of the eleven commercial wineries in the state. (See Grundy County later in this section and Montgomery County in the Heartlands section for additional fruit-of-the-vine experiences.) Open Monday through Saturday and on selected Sundays for tours and tasting; (615) 879–9519.

Overton County

In the heart of the Upper Cumberland region, Livingston, the county seat, is rapidly becoming known for its quality crafts outlets. The downtown area around the historic courthouse is known as Court Square and is the home of many retail shops, antique stores, and crafts stores.

The largest of these is the 6,000-square-foot ⊃**Court Square Emporium.** With a minimum of thirty exhibitors at any one time, the place represents a major home-based manufacturing concern that produces one-of-a-kind local products.

As renovation of the square area continues, current shop owners are optimistic that more establishments will be opened, making the area a stronger draw for those searching for Tennessee mountain crafts. Currently most of the stores are open daily except Sunday.

With a state as full of outdoor recreational facilities as Tennessee, it's difficult to call one facility unique, but the **Bend of the River Shooting Center** could well be. Located on Highway 136 about 10 miles north of Cookeville in the county's southwest section, the 100-acre center offers pistol and archery shooting ranges, a high-power-rifle range, and skeet and trap fields. In the rustic lodge, a variety of classes in shooting and firearm safety are held.

Owner Charlie Pardue welcomes shooters, "wanna-be" shooters, and spectators. If you don't have any weapons with you, you can rent a bow or gun for $3.00 a day, and shoot all you want for an additional $4.00. Ammunition is extra, of course. It's free if you just want to watch, and Charlie will lend you a pair of ear protectors. Open Saturdays only; (615) 498–2829. Charlie also owns the **Bend of the River Shooting Supply store,** 115 W. Broad Street in nearby Cookeville, where supplies can be purchased during the week; (615) 526–1136.

On your way to Cumberland County, make sure you drive through Overton's small Mennonite community in **Muddy Pond.** Off Highway 164, in the deep southeast portion of the county, you'll be able to watch true craftsmen create fine horse-drawn buggies and wagons and the harnesses and saddles to go with them. Several homes along the rural routes sell breads, pies, and eggs. Just look for the signs and stop by. If you buy a few products, chances are the people will be happy to tell you about their peaceful lives in this almost hidden community.

Cumberland County

If you're into Hank Williams, Jr., make sure you stop by the **Hank Williams Jr. General Store and Tourist Information Center,** just off Interstate 40 at the Highway 127 Exit. To be more exact, it's near Crossville, 110 miles east of Nashville and 70 miles west of Knoxville. It's located on the north side of I-40 in a funky-looking, western town lineup of buildings.

Talk about an eclectic you-won't-find-this-stuff-anywhere-else selection of things to buy! There are literally thousands of things here with Bocephus's name, picture, or logo emblazoned upon. Keychains, mugs, shirts, back scratchers, hats, kerchiefs—you name it! It's a real hoot to walk among the items and wonder what kind of a person would buy such things.

They also have snacks, and a lot of tourist information that you'll find especially helpful if you're heading toward Nashville. Open daily, year-round; 7:00 A.M. to 10:00 P.M. May through September; 8:00 A.M. to 7:00 P.M. October through April; (615) 484–4914.

Amy Brissler, owner of ⊃**Talavera De La Reina** (Tavern of the Queen), the most unusual eatery in this county, was born and raised in rural Overton County, went to Hollywood in 1935, and mingled with the stars for about forty years. When she decided it was time to come home, she retired to the land she owned out "in the wilds of Tennessee."

On that land she started to build the restaurant of her dreams piece by piece, as money would allow. In fact, that piecemeal approach is one of the factors that makes this establishment unique. She got the walls up, but superstar Marie McDonald had to supply the money to put the roof on.

Although the food is excellent, it's only part of the dining experience. Brissler, known around here as "the Queen," was one of the best costume designers in the film and television industries. Some of her creations, including dresses made for Mae West, Marilyn Monroe, Judy Garland, and a cape she made for Liberace, hang in the restaurant. She worked on one of the gowns worn by Vivien Leigh in *Gone With the Wind,* and a replica of that dress, made from the original bolt of material, is also on display.

Memorabilia, sketches from her own work, and autographed photos line the walls, and a portrait that Brissler painted of her friend Mae West hangs over the bar.

Talavera is officially a private club, but it is open for lunch and dinner to the public with advance reservations. The meals are gourmet. Call ahead to see what she's serving the day you want to be there. Two days before that date, call and order your meal. To find the Queen's kingdom, go out Interstate 40, west of Crossville, to exit 311. Go 1 mile south on Plateau Road; then 1 mile west on Highway 70; then 3 miles north on Jim Garrett Road. (615) 277–3749.

South of Crossville, where Highways 127 and 68 split, is the planned community of ⊃**Homesteads.** The area, with its quaint little stone houses lining both highways, is often referred to as the "showplace of the New Deal."

In January 1934, following several years of hard times in the area, the local farm agent submitted an application to the government for one of the subsistence projects formulated by the Roosevelt administration. The application was accepted and work began on the 10,000-acre project.

The plan was to build 250 homesteads, each of about twenty acres. The homesteaders were selected following a series of intense background checks and interviews of about 4,000 applicants. Cooperatives were established for the community, and

43

family members went to these to make their family's mattresses, can their family's food, or weave at a loom house.

Today, most of the homes are still standing and can be seen from atop the 80-foot-tall octagonal tower that originally served as a water tower. At the base is a sandstone building that housed the administrative offices of the project. Today those offices serve as a museum depicting Roosevelt's homesteading project. If you want, you can climb the ninety-seven steps to the top of the tower.

Of the 102 New Deal projects, the Cumberland Homesteads was considered one of the most, if not the most, successful of all. Admission to the museum and art gallery is free, but if you climb the tower, it will cost you 50 cents. Open daily except Wednesday; (615) 456–9663.

In addition to the museum, tower, and original homesteads, the area also has an interesting country store right across the street from the tower. Claiming to sell "Goods in Endless Variety for Man & Beast," the Cumberland General store specializes in new old-fashioned items for the modern-day homesteader. One of the best areas of the store, however, is a book section that sells how-to-books on such lost arts as hog butchering, building a stone fence, and hand digging a well. Open daily; (615) 484–8481.

Rhea County

It's hard to believe that Dayton, a small city 40 miles north of Chattanooga, was probably a household word from coast to coast during the long, hot summer of 1925. That's when the silver-tongued orators, William Jennings Bryan and Clarence Darrow, engaged in a legal battle in the ⊃**Rhea County Courthouse.** The Scopes "Monkey Trial" let the world know that a Dayton outside of Ohio actually did exist. Although John Scopes, a schoolteacher, didn't reach the heights that the Wright brothers of the other Dayton did, he earned himself a place in history.

The courthouse has been restored to its 1925 vintage and now houses a small museum in its basement. There you'll find newspaper clippings, photos, and actual newsreel footage of what many still call the first major trial treated as a media event.

Scopes was accused of teaching the Darwinian theory of evolution to a high school biology class in violation of a recently

The New Deal Homesteads Tower

passed Tennessee statute making it unlawful "to teach any theory that denies the story of the divine creation of man as taught in the Bible."

Scopes wasn't even the school's regular biology teacher, but a math teacher filling in. He was fined $100, a fee he never paid. Open Monday through Friday, during courthouse hours; admission free; (615) 775–7801.

Like strawberries? If so, plan your visit to the Dayton area during the first week of May. That's when the annual **Strawberry Festival** takes place, featuring the "World's Longest Strawberry Shortcake" and fourteen days of eclectic fun.

Other events include a carnival midway full of rides, a formal ball, various sports tournaments, an arts and crafts show, and the Strawberry Jam, a music festival. (615) 775–0361.

To get to Meigs County, follow Highway 30 out of Dayton until it disappears into the Tennessee River. If you're lucky, your timing will get you there as the ⊃**Washington Ferry** is loading. If not, there's never much of a wait.

In operation since 1807, the $^1/_3$-mile trek across the river is one of the four oldest operating ferry routes in the U.S. There has been a major debate in the area since about 1927 as to where to build a bridge. "Until they figure out where to build that bridge, we'll be in business," said ferry owner Charles Smith. There's another ferry about 10 miles downriver on Highway 60.

The eight-car boat takes less than five minutes to cross the river and costs $2.00 per vehicle. If you have to wait, take a minute and ask the fishermen at the ferry slip how the fish are biting. You may end up in a conversation so interesting you won't mind if you miss your boat. There's no night operation across the river; it operates year-round. (615) 775–3857.

Meigs County

Continue on Highway 30, and you'll come to the small county seat community of Decatur, where an historic town square will attract your attention. Unlike many of the older courthouse squares, this one is a bit barren and free of large trees.

But in the shadow of the courthouse, you'll find the area's version of the ⊃**Spit and Whittle Gang,** a bunch of old-timers who gather each day to—well, you guessed it.

Over behind the post office, on tiny Smith Avenue, is the **Meigs County Historical Museum.** Housed in an 1880s Gothic building, the interior has been restored to its natural wooden glory. In 1948, the last of several attorneys who practiced their trade here hung his shingle over the front door.

Dudley Culvahouse served the area for many years before retiring. After his "official" retirement, he still worked with a few clients and wrote wills and other documents for those who needed them. He became famous for the sign that hung in his doorway for years. It read: "Open when I get here. Closed when I get tired."

That sign is now hanging in the museum. Upon his death in 1989, his widow sold the building to the historical society. "The building was built by a Smith, and it's located on Smith Avenue," said one of the volunteers who runs it. "So we refer to our museum as the Little Smithsonian."

Full of local memorabilia and artifacts, the museum is open Thursdays and Fridays, 10:00 A.M. to 2:00 P.M., and other days by request. If you want to see inside, and there aren't any volunteers on duty, call the phone number that's posted on the door, and that "on-call" volunteer will come down and show you around.

Outside of town, in the middle of the Tennessee River, is **Jolley's Island,** where Sam Houston lived with the Cherokee Indians for several years and earned his Indian name, "The Raven." The National Park Service plans to make the island an official part of the Trail of Tears.

The island, which can be seen from the Blythe Ferry (located south of the Washington Ferry), will house several historical exhibits, including a marble wall with the names of the Native Americans who left on the Trail of Tears journey.

McMinn County

In Athens, just off Highway 30, rests Tennessee Wesleyan College, a liberal arts school established in 1857. The first building on campus, appropriately called the "Old College" building, is still standing and up until 1989 housed the county's heritage museum.

The structure, built in 1854 and also used as a hospital during the Civil War, faces the quad grounds of the school. Behind Old

College, on Dwain Farmer Drive, you'll find a marker explaining one of the most poignant legends in Tennessee history.

A wounded English officer from nearby Fort Loudon was befriended by an Indian chief and nursed back to health by Nocatula, daughter of the chief. The soldier, given the name of Connestoga (the oak), was accepted into the tribe and married Nocatula. A jealous suitor attacked Connestoga with a knife. As he lay dying, Nocatula confessed her eternal love for him and plunged a knife into her breast.

The pair were buried together, and the chief placed an acorn in Connestoga's hand and a hackberry in Nocatula's hand, symbolizing undying love. From these there developed two trees that grew intertwined on this spot for more than 150 years.

After these two original trees died in 1957, two others were planted. Those have since died, and today the stumps are all that remain.

The ⊃**McMinn County Living Heritage Museum** moved out of the Old College building in late 1989 and moved to the city's old high school building, about a half-mile from downtown at 522 W. Madison Avenue.

The museum's collection of nineteenth- and twentieth-century quilts is one of the finest in the state. In addition to the permanent display of quilts, a nationally known quilt show is hosted by the museum each February, March, and April.

There is also a great children's collection that includes china and bisque-head dolls, toys, and clothing, along with school desks, books, and maps dating from 1850. Admission is charged; open daily but closed on major holidays; (615) 745–0329.

Polk County

If you happen to be in this part of the state and are tired of beautiful, lush mountains and forests, trek on over to the Ducktown area, a portion of the state often referred to as ⊃**Tennessee's Badlands.**

Here you won't be surrounded by lush, green vegetation. In fact, you'll be surrounded by a 56-square-mile area of barren red hills, stunted pine trees, and washed-out gullies. This area of raw landscape is similar in looks to the famed badlands area of the Dakotas.

Geographically, the area is known as the Copper Basin and was the site of a thriving copper-mining industry that lasted 144 years, ending on July 31, 1987.

Intensive reforestation has made a big dent in the destruction, but in 1978 local residents made a move to put an end to the reforestation efforts and to preserve the area as a unique part of Tennessee's history. Today, the **Ducktown Basin Museum** has been opened not only to preserve various artifacts and memorabilia of the mining operations but also to educate people about what went on in this corner of the state.

The museum is located on thirteen acres of the former Burra Burra Mine site, now a national designated historic district, in the community of Ducktown, just off Highway 64. It was organized in 1983 and has been "run on a shoestring" ever since, according to Bobbie Jean Beckler, a leader of the movement to preserve the basin area.

Inside the museum you'll find a great many photos, maps, copper ore samples, and the various tools of the trade. Since the total demise of the industry was predated by efforts to preserve it, a true, complete representation of the area is on display, or soon will be. You'll also have a pretty good shot at meeting one of the people who worked the mines, who will be able to give you a firsthand account of the operation.

Jim Cole, whose family worked in the area for generations, is an accomplished carver, and his work, depicting people working the tasks of the industry, are on display in the museum. These carvings are great examples of Tennessee folk art.

Tours are given through the various Burra Burra buildings Monday through Saturday during the winter, plus Sundays during the summer. If you want to see a part of Tennessee that most of the state's residents don't even know exists, here's your chance. It has to be the most overlooked, historically significant area in the entire state. Admission is charged; (615) 496–5778.

Farther down Highway 64, between Ducktown and Cleveland, you'll find yourself driving along the Ocoee River, one of the top ten white-water rivers in the country. You'll also find numerous business establishments that will be more than happy to rent you a raft, canoe, or kayak so you too can experience an adventure of a lifetime.

If you're not of the adventurous variety or don't have the time, there are several pull-offs where you can experience the dangers and the excitement vicariously. The mostly two-lane road is very busy here, so be careful to pull off the road completely before looking too much.

Look closely through the trees on the other side of the river and you'll see the largest wooden flume known to exist in the United States. The ⊃**Ocoee Flume** is 5 miles long, 11 feet wide, and 14 feet tall. Originally built in 1912 by the Tennessee Valley Authority (TVA), it was closed for a few years in the late 1970s and was rebuilt.

Its major function is to divert water from the river to help produce hydroelectric power, but recently it has also been a savior of the river for the white-water aficionados. With the diversion the flume creates, the TVA can produce their power and the river can still run to the point of whiteness.

Bradley County

Mention mountain forests and fantastic views, and most people think of the Smoky Mountains. That's why the 620,000-acre ⊃**Cherokee National Forest** here in the southeast portion of the state remains virtually untouched by crowds.

More than 1,100 miles of roads have been cut through the dense forest, opening up all sorts of opportunities for outdoor enthusiasts or for those who simply enjoy driving and looking. Take your time; there's a real good chance that no one will be honking and trying to get around you. The Forest Service maintains twenty-nine camping areas, horse trails (bring your own horse), and 105 hiking trails. This area is every bit as beautiful as the Smokies, making it a great alternative that most locals are hesitant to tell too many people about. The supervisor's office can give you more specifics; (615) 338–5201.

About 6 miles outside Cleveland on Highway 64E, hidden behind the hustle and bustle of a busy highway and myriad antique shops and flea markets, is a neat little living-history museum called the ⊃**Primitive Settlement.** Here, a collection of nineteenth-century log cabins from the area has been moved and rebuilt to show life the way it was. The owners claim that they have the area's largest collection of primitive antiques.

When you enter the gates, the settlement appears to be a small attraction, but once you start talking with the employees and sticking your head into the various corners, a visit can turn into a very interesting couple of hours. Each cabin, with the oldest being more than 150 years old, depicts a different mode of frontier life.

During the summer, live country music is offered every Saturday night. Open daily March through October; admission is charged; (615) 476–5096.

About 12 miles south of Cleveland, off a series of back roads, you'll find the historic ⊃**Red Clay** area. Red Clay was the site of the last council ground of the Cherokee Indian nation before their forced removal in 1838. It was the site of eleven general councils, national affairs attended by up to 5,000 Indians each.

The U.S. government wanted the Cherokees to surrender their eastern lands and move the entire tribe to lands in Oklahoma. The Cherokees fought it for quite a while, but controversial treaties resulted in their losing the land. Here at Red Clay, the journey to Oklahoma, known today as the Trail of Tears, actually began.

The march, often referred to as the Great Removal, was a wintertime, cross-country journey that covered more than 1,000 miles. Reportedly, 4,000 of the 18,000 who were forced to leave perished during the walk. That was almost one-fourth of the entire Cherokee nation.

Today, people can drive that same path across the state on the "Trail of Tears State Historic Route." It's marked quite well, and maps that explain the various historical activities along the way are available here at Red Clay. About 80 percent of the original trail is now covered by modern highways.

Here where it all began a 275-acre state historic area has been developed. The only original part left is the council spring, locally known as the "blue hole." It was this pure running spring that probably attracted the Cherokees to this site in the first place.

Also on the grounds are various reproductions of early Indian homesteads and an interpretive center with displays and historical exhibits.

It's not an easy place to find. Take Highway 60 south out of Cleveland and follow the signs. They are good signs but often understated in size and can be easily overlooked if you happen to be looking at the cows and horses along the way. If you see a sign that reads "Welcome to Georgia," you've gone about a half-mile too far. Open daily; admission free; (615) 478–0339.

Hamilton County

Chattanooga, the state's fourth largest city, with a population of less than 200,000 is located along a 7-mile bend in the Tennessee River. The deep ravine along the river is often referred to as the Grand Canyon of the South.

Lookout Mountain is probably the best known of the three major "ledges" that loom over the city. And, as in any major tourist destination, the beaten path and the unbeaten path catch up with each other here, with the same attraction often offering different things to different people.

A lot of states have large public aquariums, but none can beat the ꙨTennessee Aquarium here in Chattanooga, at One Broad Street, next to the Tennessee River. The location is quite appropriate for the theme of this beautiful facility, which opened in late May, 1992.

Billed as the "world's first major freshwater life center," the aquarium salutes the state that has more species of freshwater fish than any other state. Few of us will ever have the chance to personally explore the entire length of the magnificent Tennessee River, but here's your chance, and it will take less than two hours.

Through exhibits of live and luxuriant flora and fauna, you can take a journey from the river's source in the Appalachian High Country through its midstream and finally to the Mississippi Delta. A visit to the aquarium is an enjoyable experience for the entire family. Open every day except Christmas and Thanksgiving. Admission charged; (615) 265–0695.

Along with all its Civil War history, the area around Lookout Mountain contains a lesser-known fact about an earlier war. History books usually tell us that the American Revolution started at Lexington and ended with Cornwallis's surrender at Yorktown. Actually, historians currently say that the last engagement between official forces of the war took place on the slopes of Lookout Mountain on September 20, 1782, a year after Yorktown.

The National Park Service must agree with these historians, because they have marked the spot, just off Highway 148 near the foot of the mountain, with a historical marker, calling it the Ꙩ"Last Battle of the Revolution."

Farther up the mountain, one of the Civil War's most famous battles was fought. Known today as the "Battle Above the Clouds," the fight at Chickamauga Creek and the Battle of

Chattanooga are immortalized in the nation's first and largest national military park. The huge **Chickamauga–Chattanooga National Park,** established in 1890, contains more than 400 markers on the battlefield, outlining the series of events that claimed 34,000 casualties. In addition, the park also contains 666 monuments honoring the men who fought on the grounds.

The visitors center is a good place to start your education on the area's Civil War history. It's located at the top of the mountain across from the entrance to Point Park, the site of the "Battle Above the Clouds." (615) 821-7786.

As you climb the mountain, you'll pass several other well-known attractions, including the incredible **Ruby Falls.** They are very much on the beaten path but shouldn't be overlooked just because you don't like crowds or don't want to visit a place just because everyone else in the world has been there first. (615) 821-2544.

Many Tennessee natives don't realize that one of the most popular attractions on Lookout Mountain, **Rock City,** is actually across the state line in Georgia.

"See Rock City" birdhouses and painted barn roofs throughout the Southeast have made this attraction a genuine piece of Americana. There's nothing like it anywhere else. Ten acres of natural rock gardens, some with formations looming twenty stories high, and a barren spot called Lover's Leap, where seven states can be seen, are the highlights of the attraction. Twisting paths take you through wonderfully landscaped gardens and narrow crevices. One such crack is thoughtfully named "Fat Man's Squeeze."

The founder, Garnet Carter, first built a hotel on the property and in early 1928 developed a recreational outlet that changed leisure-time activities from coast to coast. Using the natural hills, rocks, hollow logs, and pools of water as hazards, he created a miniature golf course for his guests who didn't want to take the time to play a complete round of regulation golf.

Within a short time, various other hotels in the country asked him to design courses for them, and "Tom Thumb Golf" took the country by storm. By 1930 about 25,000 miniature golf courses were operating in the United States, many of which were Carter's courses.

The original course and the hotel are now gone, but several of the small characters that were placed around the course are now

53

A Rock City Barn

a part of the Fairyland portion of Rock City. Admission is charged; (404) 820–2531.

Less than a mile from Rock City, at the very top of the mountain, **The Castle in the Clouds** resort hotel was built in 1928. Today the old hotel, since restored, is the main building for Covenant College, a small liberal arts school. Other buildings on the campus also have historical as well as nostalgic appeal. Drop by and look up one of the school's officials, who love to give tours. (404) 820–1560.

If you're a little leery about driving up the mountain, there's a solution. Built in 1895, the **Lookout Mountain Incline** is now a part of the city's transit system. Billed as the "World's Steepest and Safest Incline Railway," it has a 72.7-percent grade near the top. At the top of the mile-long ride, the upper station has been developed into a small retail village, which happens to have the best ice cream in the Chattanooga area. (615) 821–4224.

Pardon me boy, but let's go visit the ↻**Chattanooga Choo Choo.** Down in the city, the Choo Choo is one of the most unusual shopping areas in the state. Located at the old Terminal Station, the complex features a Holiday Inn with rooms in restored train cars, landscaped gardens, and myriad Victorian-era shops and restaurants. All play on the train theme. 1400 Market Street; (800) TRACK–29.

The city was one of the country's earliest and largest railroad centers, and this station was the hub of that activity. On the top floor of one of the terminal buildings, one of the world's largest model railroad layouts has been created by a local model railroad club showing the area as it was during the heyday. During the week it can be seen running under automated control, but on weekends members of the club come out and "play" with their creation.

The entire display is 174 feet long and contains more than 3,000 square feet of space. The HO-gauge layout has about 100 locomotives and several hundred passenger and freight cars on about 100 miles of track. Admission charged.

Several stores sell 45-RPM records of Glenn Miller's version of the Chattanooga Choo Choo song. The phrase itself was coined in 1880 when a reporter took the first train ride out of Cincinnati on the new Cincinnati-Southern Line. Since the tracks only went as far as this city, he called the train the "Chattanooga Choo Choo."

Chattanooga Choo Choo

Before leaving the city, another interesting stop is the **National Knife Museum.** Owned and operated by the National Knife Collectors Association, the 8,000-square-foot museum was created to provide a showplace for the work of the association's 16,000 members. Private collections from members are on display, as is the museum's growing permanent collection. Handmade blades and knives from most of the 360 American cutlery firms are featured. By the way, one thing you'll find out here is that a knife collector is technically known as a *machairologist.* The museum is located at 7201 Shallowford Road, at I–75. Admission charged. Open Monday through Saturday; (615) 892–5007.

Leave Chattanooga via Highway 41/64/72, also known as Will Cummings Highway, toward Raccoon Mountain. As you approach the mountain, you'll see signs for **High Adventure Sport,** located at 4117 Cummings Highway, across from the Highway Patrol station. There you'll see the state's best area for hang gliding. If you aren't inclined to fly yourself, there are several places to watch others. The park also has the world's first hang-gliding simulator, by which one can experience the feeling without actually being thrown off a mountain. Bungee jumping, from a 176-foot-high platform, is also offered. (615) 825–0444.

Marion County

Farther up Highway 41 just across the county line on your right, you'll see the sign for the ⊃TVA's **Raccoon Mountain Pumped Storage Facility.** It is the most unusual of all the Tennessee Valley Authority's operations.

This hydroelectric plant uses more power than it generates. The safety officers who take you on an amazing hour-long tour of the plant will usually agree with that arguable fact, but they will quickly tell you that the plant is very cost-effective.

The visitors center is located at the top of the mountain, about 9 miles from the front entrance, and what a view of the Tennessee River Valley it offers! Also at the top is a 528-acre lake. Deep inside the mountain is the mammoth power plant, totally protected from the elements and enemy attack.

At night, during off-peak hours, the extra energy produced at TVA coal-burning plants is used here to pump water from the Tennessee River up a 1,100-foot pipeline to fill the reservoir above. This is cheaper than shutting down and restarting those plants, and the electricity that would be wasted is now used to "stockpile" water that will in turn create more power.

During the day, when the demand for electricity is greatest, the water is released from the reservoir and tumbles down the 35-foot diameter intake tunnels to turn the four large generators, thereby producing electricity.

During the free tour, the guide will take you through some of the 2¼ miles of bored-out tunnels within the mountain. Also, you'll visit one of the cavernlike rooms, each large enough to hold twelve tennis courts and with ceilings 80 feet tall. The statistics recited to you will boggle your mind.

There are fewer than two dozen pumped storage facilities in the United States, and this is the only one that is completely underground. There are several scenic pull-offs on the drive to the top and quite a few picnic areas. At the foot of the mountain, there are fishing areas along the river, all courtesy of the Federal government. Tours are given daily; admission free; (615) 751-2420.

As you pull back out onto Highway 41, take a right and head toward the best catfish dinner or lunch you've ever had. About 6 miles from the TVA, and in a different time zone, you'll find the

Ↄ**Riverside Catfish House** on Highway 41 North on the right next to the river.

The family-run business was established in 1959 and is owned today by Miss Hattie Massengale. Daughters Linda Turner, Sharon Graves, and Donna Caradine work there, as does Turner's daughter. The place seats 125, with many of the tables in front of big windows overlooking the river. "We don't take reservations, so you'll have to get here early if you want a window seat," cautions Turner.

Although they also serve items other than fish, Turner said that 95 percent of the people order the grain-fed catfish dinner, which comes with coleslaw and hush puppies. (In the lobby, there's a picture of a cow and a pig, both begging the patrons to "Please eat Fish.") If you enjoy a cold beer with your catfish, you're out of luck here. "We used to sell it, but the church people complained," Turner said. For dessert, Miss Hattie's famous buttermilk pie is a favorite, as is Turner's cheesecake.

They're open Thursday through Sunday, and although they are on central time, they run by eastern time since most of their customers come from "that side of the line." (615) 821–9214.

Grundy County

In Tracy City, you'll find Ↄ**Dutch Maid Bakery,** the state's oldest family bakery. Along with its baked goods, the store sells a nice selection of local crafts, a sampling of local honey, and other "cottage industry" products made in this area of the state.

Founded by John Baggenstoss in 1902, the bakery is still owned and run by family members. Through the years all of Baggenstoss's six sons have been involved in the family business, but today the operation is in the hands of a cousin.

The bakery resembles a museum. Everything but the merchandise is at least sixty years old, and most of the baking is done in a 1930s converted stoker oven.

In addition to their famous applesauce fruitcake, the bakers also create salt-rising bread and other "regular" bakery items. Informal tours are given whenever someone drops in and wants one. Open daily; (615) 592–3171. Make sure you get on the mailing list so you can order by mail.

Stay on Highway 41 and head to Monteagle, where, just across

Interstate 24 on Highway 64/41A, you'll find one of the best places for pit barbecue and hickory-smoked meats in the state. **Jim Oliver's Smokehouse** complex offers a great country store, meeting rooms, a lodge, a motel, and his famous restaurant. In all, he has twenty acres, full of all sorts of things to do. The motel's swimming pool is a sight in itself: it's in the shape of a ham. (615) 924–2268.

Across the highway is the **Monteagle Wine Cellars,** which offers tours and wine tasting. The establishment of the winery here represents what is hoped to be a revitalization of the area's grape growing and wine making that was started by a group of Swiss immigrants who settled nearby in 1870. Monteagle is at an elevation of 2,100 feet. Open daily year-round; (615) 924–2120.

If you're heading toward Monteagle, make plans to stay at the **Edgeworth Inn,** located on the grounds of the historic Monteagle Assembly. The inn, owned and operated by Wendy and David Adams, is a first-class, ten-bedroom bed and breakfast. Built as a boardinghouse in 1896, the structure has been completely renovated to its Victorian splendor and offers guests a respite from the real world.

Each morning you'll find Wendy and David in the kitchen baking the day's breakfast, which includes carrot muffins, spoon bread, sausage casserole, and a selection of the Adams' specialty breads. While here, you'll eat from Wedgwood china, cover up with heirloom quilts, and get a chance to enjoy the family's extensive art collection located throughout the house.

The Adamses accept no pets, and they ask you to call ahead and make arrangements if you'll be bringing children. Rooms start at $55. (615) 924–2669.

Grundy County is gaining a national reputation as a mountain crafts center, thanks to several artisans whose works are known and in demand from coast to coast. Many of these craftspeople have settled in the center of the county and have established homes and local ties.

In Altamont, woodcarver Ron Van Dyke bought the town's old mill and has rebuilt a couple of its buildings and has plans to restore as much as possible. Greeters Mill pumped water for the town, ground its corn, cut its wood, and was a major operation until 1968.

Today, one of the buildings serves as the home for the **Cumberland Craftsman,** a shop specializing in Van Dyke's work as well as that of other local artists. The old wood kiln is now Van Dyke's workshop. Out front, the old steam engine that was used in this operation has been put back together and painted. It's a good landmark for the establishment. Make sure you take a look at his claim to fame, the Hillbilly Chess Set. This hand-carved set features Pa (king), Ma with rolling pin (queen), the boys, with rifles (knights), whiskey barrels (pawns), stills (bishops), and out-houses (castles). (615) 692-3595.

As you head north on Highway 56, you'll see the ⊃**Old Wood Village** just before you enter the village of Beersheba Springs. Proprietor William Hassel has moved three old buildings from the area to his property and uses them to live in, work in, and showcase his crafts. After doing the craft-show circuit for about ten years, Hassel decided to quit the rat race and move to Tennessee. While on the juried show route, he earned himself a national reputation for his woodwork.

Among his works, he features various pieces of furniture that combine the art of fine woodworking with mountain twig designs. He also creates and carves out wooden vessels that are shaped like urns and bowls.

Hassel is usually in his shop trying to keep up with the demand of being a one-person business, but he'll always take time to sit down and chat with you about his business or the simple life of Grundy County. (615) 692-3829.

On the other side of Beersheba Springs, Phil and Terri Mayhew live and work in an 1850s log cabin. Phil's work with high-fired, functional porcelain pottery is represented by sixteen galleries in twelve states. Terri creates porcelain and hand-wrought silver jewelry. Phil, a former arts professor, has developed a porcelain that will fuse at a higher temperature, thus making it more durable and giving it a unique color range. Phil and Terri both will show you their work, usually displayed on the front porch of their house during the warmer months. Their business is called **Beersheba Porcelain.** (615) 692-2280.

Beersheba Springs was a bustling resort area during the last half of the 1800s; and its grand hotel, which was built in 1850, is still standing. Down the road a couple of blocks from the Mayhews, the building is now owned by the United Methodist Church and used as a summer meeting facility. The view from the front of the hotel is nothing less than breathtaking.

When the hotel was active, stagecoaches would stop at the foot of the mountain and sound a horn once for each guest they had aboard for the hotel. By the time they reached the top, the hotel's band was ready to greet them. Dinner and a clean room had also been prepared.

The hotel grounds are the site of an annual arts and crafts show held in late August.

Sequatchie County

High atop Fredonia Mountain, down a series of gravel roads, Greg and Lisa Warren have named their home and acreage **⊃Rivendell Farm.** If you're a J. R. R. Tolkien fan, you'll recognize Rivendell as the name of a valley in *The Lord of the Rings*.

"That's where all the elves lived," said Greg. "Now, llamas live here instead." Greg and Lisa have fourteen of them and are in the llama-raising business. Their private stock is used for packing and trail rides as well as pets. The Warrens also raise spotted saddlebred horses, a breed that is rapidly gaining in popularity. It's too hard to give directions to the farm, but Greg said to call him first and he'd tell you how to get there; (615) 949–3868.

Down the mountain in Dunlap, there's a developing historic site that most overlook, mainly because it was the illegal town dump for decades. Through the dedication of volunteers, headed up by Carson Camp, history is being uncovered on the sixty-two-acre **⊃Coke Ovens Historic Site.**

A huge coal industry was present in this area at the turn of the century, and in this Dunlap industrial complex coal was turned into coke for use in the iron and steel foundries in nearby Chattanooga.

When the company went out of business in 1917, there were 268 beehive-shaped coke ovens in operation. Through the years, the ovens were forgotten, covered up, and neglected. During the past few years, Camp and his crew have uncovered a lot of the area's heritage that had almost been forgotten.

The park has been listed on the National Register of Historic Places, and a museum is being built on the original foundation of the old commissary building. Excavation is continuing; meanwhile the park is open, and on some days you might find Camp or one of his volunteers over in a corner with a shovel in hand. They'll tell you the story. (615) 949–3483.

61

Warren County

⊃**Cumberland Caverns,** located about 7 miles southeast of McMinnville on Highway 8, is the second largest cavern system in the United States, after Kentucky's Mammoth Cave. Unless you happen to be an expert in this sort of thing, most of the tour through the cave reminds you of just about any other cave journey.

One room here, however, is impressive no matter what your interests are. The "Hall of the Mountain King" room is 600 feet long, 150 feet wide, and 140 feet high. It is the largest cave room east of the Mississippi River. The room's man-made amenities are built alongside the natural formations. Of these constructed features, the most amazing is the dining room, which will seat 500 for a banquet. High above the tables is a 15-foot, 1,500-pound chandelier from a theater in Brooklyn, New York.

Also in this room, one will see (and hear) a theater pipe organ and a stage equipped for live shows or movies. And all this is more than 300 feet below the hustle and bustle of the real world above! (615) 668–4396.

Cannon County

Cannon County is known throughout the state for the number of fine craftsmen it has within its borders. Just about every craft you can think of is created here by a superb artist. From potters to folk artists to basket weavers to chair makers, a great many craftsmen call Cannon County home.

Unfortunately, most of the gifted craftspeople don't like you to visit their home workshops unless they know you, preferring instead to sell their crafts through various shops and at craft shows throughout the Southeast. Once you do business with them at a show, they'll probably let you do business directly with them from their home.

The county's craftspeople come out in force for the local White Oak Country Fair, held the second weekend in August. Artists from other counties are invited to participate as well, making this a wonderful place to buy unique items you won't find in too many locales.

Sponsored by the **Cannon Association of Craft Artists,**

the juried show is in its infancy and as it grows, the date and location may change accordingly. Check statewide crafts show calendars or write the association at P.O. Box 27, Woodbury 37190. Or call Priscilla Woodward, one of the organizers of the event, at (615) 563–4619.

Up off Highway 96 at the very top of the county is the little community of Auburntown, which claims to have the "Best Little Fish Fry in the South." A tradition that started in 1978 to raise money for the local Lion's Club, the event is the social highlight of the area. Held the first Saturday night of each month in the community center, the dinner is just about the best bargain around, especially if you're hungry.

The Lion's Club outing was so popular that the local fire department decided to fry up some fish on their own. Held the *third* Saturday of each month, the firefighters' fry offers the same menu, at the same price, in the same location. Business is brisk both nights.

For $6, you get all the great northern white bass you can eat, along with hush puppies, coleslaw, and iced tea or coffee. There's a huge repeat business from month to month from a five- or six-county radius. It's a great place to catch up on all the gossip.

Dekalb County

The Herndons are having a swine time out on Blue Springs Road, about 8 miles south of Smithville. Jimmy and Fran run ϽH & H Pig Farm, a farrow-to-finish pig operation.

Several years ago when they first got the idea, they went to the University of Tennessee for advice. They listened to what the folks told them, and from the building plans to the type of lights to use, they followed all the advice to the inch. Today the operation is one of the most efficient pig facilities in the state.

Tennessee is eighteenth in the United States in hog production, but agriculture as a whole is the state's number-one employment, employing about 25 percent of the state's population. More than 80 percent of the state's land is used, in one form or another, for agriculture.

The Herndons' operation turns out about 2,000 pigs a year from their 100-sow herd. Fran will show you around the farm and explain the whole process, from hand breeding to birthing to nursery time to finishing to shipping. The length of time from birth to market is usually less than six months. (615) 597–7303.

Putnam County

Cookeville, this county's seat of government, had two early surges of commerce that resulted in two distinctive downtown sections. The town had already established its square and business hub long before the railroads came through. When the rails came to town in 1890, they came through a residential area on the west side of town. That area soon became less residential and more commercial as business shifted from the established area around the courthouse to the new, prospering area around the depot. A large hotel was built, and warehouses and stores soon followed.

By 1910 a new passenger depot had been built, and the area was considered the "Hub of the Upper Cumberland." Passenger service was terminated in 1955, but the locals were able to save the depot, now on the National Register of Historic Places and the site of the ⊃**Cookeville Depot Museum.**

Inside is one of the best re-creations of an early depot in the state. Original fixtures, desks, time schedules, and the like have been preserved through the years. There are four rooms of exhibits, plus a caboose out back with more displays. Admission is free; location is Broad and Cedar streets; (615) 528–5550.

Across the street from the museum, high atop an old dairy, you'll see a big, old-fashioned neon sign advertising Cream City Ice Cream. Atop the sign is a giant ice cream sundae whose cherry bounces up and down (in neon) when the sign is turned on. The people who bought the location when the dairy closed chose to not only save but restore the sign to its 1950s beauty. Now, several times each year, the sign is lit, much to the delight of local photographers and nostalgia buffs.

If that makes you hungry, drop by **Diana's Bakery** at 104 East Spring Street. She has taken a century-old home and converted it into a six-room restaurant, open for lunch Monday through Saturday, and daily at 7:30 A.M. for continental breakfast. Specialties include her famous chicken pot pies, quiches, crab salad, and various deli sandwiches. To live up to her slogan that her eatery has "The Sweetest Buns in Town," fresh-baked cinnamon and pecan rolls are also offered.

Plan to drop by in midmorning before the local lunch crowd comes in, grab a bun and a coffee, and head out to the veranda to enjoy the scenery. (615) 526–6967.

Clay County

In Celina, one will find the oldest ⊃**OshKosh B'Gosh** factory in the South. OshKosh, founded in Wisconsin in 1895, is a leading manufacturer of workwear and children's apparel, with a total of sixteen Southeast plants, including ten in Tennessee. There are two plants here. The manufacturing plant, established in 1953, is the oldest of the company's facilities in the Southeast; and the 97,000-square-foot finishing plant, built in 1991, is the company's newest facility in the country.

A tour of both is quite interesting, but the trip through the finishing plant's laundry is amazing. This is where huge computerized washers stone wash, super bleach, and ice wash denim fabrics to give them the washed-out look so popular today. You've never seen anything like this in your local laundromat!

The manufacturing plant is located at Westlake and Mitchell streets, just west of the square, and the finishing plant is 3 miles out of town on Highway 53. The washers are almost always full, since this is the company's only finishing plant in the South. Marian Overstreet is the person who will walk you through. Give her a call in advance if possible; (615) 243–3151.

If you think marbles are just for kids, then you haven't met the gang of marble players in Celina. For the group of dedicated players around here, the simple ring marble game is unheard of. What they play in "these here" parts is called Rolley Hole.

The game is a team sport, played on a 40-foot by 20-foot field called a marbleyard. There are three holes evenly spaced down the middle. The object of the game is for each team of two to get their marbles into each hole in succession, down the court, back and down again, three times.

The top players make their own marbles or buy them from other local players. The top player was Dumas Walker, who died in 1991. He was the world champion Rolley Hole player, and people would come from miles to watch him play.

In his memory, the **Dumas Walker (King of Marbles) Tournament** is held each August in conjunction with the county's Homecoming Day celebration. Players from other Rolley Hole hotbeds, namely Kansas City and parts of New Jersey, come to Celina to compete in that tourney. In September, the national championships are held at the nearby Standing Stone State Park. Several English players usually show up for that one as well.

No one seems to know why this type of marble playing is so popular around here, but you'll see marbleyards all over town, and just about every night there will be at least one game going on. If you happen to come through town during the day, drop by the Hevi-Duty Electric shop, just outside of town. The boys working here are champion shooters and practice out back during breaks. (615) 243-3113.

The **Dale Hollow National Fish Hatchery,** just north of Celina on Highway 53, produces yearly about 200,000 pounds of 9-inch rainbow trout, which are used to restock public waterways. They also hatch and ship about 500,000 fingerlings each year.

Most of the public waterways in the Southeast are too warm for trout to breed, hence the need for this facility. Trout fishing is allowed and encouraged on most dam and river sites owned by the government, so periodic restocking is necessary.

The hatchery offers self-guided tours, but there are plenty of workers around to answer any questions. A long greenhouse-type of building is where the eggs are hatched, and then the small trout are taken outside to spend the rest of their time here in one of the sixty-four 8-foot by 100-foot concrete raceways.

Feeding times, early morning and late afternoon, are probably the best times to visit. The larger fish are fed food pellets from a truck. A certain amount of food drops down onto a base and then is blown across the water by a current of air. The smaller fish are fed by hand. Open every day year-round; admission free; (615) 243-2443.

Macon County

During the first half of this century, ↄ**Red Boiling Springs** was a bustling health and vacation resort known for its medicinal waters. The resort enjoyed its heyday in the years between the world wars, when as many as six large hotels and ten boardinghouses were in business. Today the spa resort feeling hasn't totally vanished. The springs are still here, as are three of the hotels, and you can still get a mineral water bath. A major flood in the sixties wiped out much of the old-time charm, but the community has rebuilt and has restored much of that ambience.

Armour's Red Boiling Springs Hotel, one of the survivors, has twenty-six guest rooms available for a flat fee of $30 per day per person, which includes breakfast and dinner. The inn also has the only bath house still in operation. You can "take the cure" here for $15. That includes a bath in black water and an hour treatment. (615) 699–2180.

The town was famous for four types of water: black, red, double and twist, and free stone. Each is quite different in its mineral analysis and each was considered a "cure" for different ailments. A self-guided-tour brochure of the area is available at the small log visitors center on Market Street.

Over in Lafayette, the county seat, you don't have to have a map to find the biggest loafers in the county. On any fair-weather day, be it in January or June, you'll find a group of men of indeterminate age sitting under an old oak tree on the southeast side of the Macon County Public Square. With knife in hand, these whittlers have become part of small-town life around here. The chamber of commerce likes them because of their almost unlimited knowledge of the area. But you don't have to have kin in the area to ask after; just walk right up and start talking with them. But, of course, you'll always walk away wondering whether the directions they gave you will really take you where you want to go or whether these good ole boys have played another trick on a city slicker.

About 5 miles southwest of Lafayette on Old Hartsville Pike, Buck Gammons has found a home for his extensive collection of "junk, antiques, and you name its." A collector for more than thirty years, Buck had been wanting a place to put all his stuff so he could see it all. He found a barn about 2 miles from his house and has been restoring it while stocking it to the beams with his collections.

He started collecting when he lost everything in a house fire. Now he says he can't throw anything away. One of his larger collections is of empty Maxwell House Coffee jars. He hasn't thrown one away since 1955.

He calls his barn the **Old Hartsville Pike Roadside Park and Museum.** His collection is open to the public, and he'll usually charge $2.00 per person. "I tell them if they aren't totally happy with what they see, I'll give them the money back when they leave," he contends. So far, he hasn't been asked for a refund.

Although he's officially retired, Buck still "spends too much time working," so a call before you visit would be wise; (615) 655–5460.

Off the Beaten Path in the Heartland

1. Music Row
2. Museum of Tobacco Art and History
3. Greek Parthenon
4. Museum of Beverage Containers and Advertising
5. Twitty City
6. The Carter House
7. Carnton Mansion
8. Manuel's Cajun Country Store
9. Nissan Motors Manufacturing Corporation
10. George Dickel Distillery
11. Jack Daniel's Distillery
12. Hundred Oaks Castle
13. Falls Mill
14. Carlton's General Store
15. Bell Buckle
16. Wartrace
17. Moon Pencil Company
18. Village of Hohenwald
19. Brushy Store and Cafe
20. Loretta Lynn Ranch
21. World O'Tools
22. Land Between the Lakes
23. Clarksville-Montgomery County Historical Society
24. Plummer's Old Store and Museum
25. Adams
26. Southeastern Wild Horse and Burro Adoption Center

The Heartland

Davidson County

No matter where you go in the world, mention Nashville to anyone and you'll get a smile of understanding. Ah, country music—that's what most people associate with the state's capital city.

Nashville is one of the areas where the unbeaten path crosses the well-traveled path and merges for a few miles and a dozen or so attractions.

There's no place like Nashville (a.k.a. Music City, Twangtown). Its maternal relationship to country music has created quite a few unique attractions and events. Since the majority of visitors come to see the music-associated attractions, many of the other attractions are ignored to a greater extent than they would be in just about any other city. Five of the region's top ten attractions are country music related.

A hint about getting around: There's a lot of traffic in the downtown and Music Row areas during peak summer periods, and parking spots can be hard to find. Find one and leave the driving to the Nashville Trolley Company. It's 50 cents a ride, or you can buy a book of ten tickets for $2.00. Unfortunately, the trolleys don't offer service to the outlying areas.

In the northeast quadrant of the city, home to the mammoth Opryland USA, make sure you visit the **Nashville Palace,** across the street from the entrance to the Opryland Hotel. The Palace, owned by the friendly Johnny Hobbs, is where country superstar Randy Travis was discovered while working as a dishwasher. Live music nightly and a delicious menu that includes "the best catfish in town" are featured. (615) 885–1540.

The world famous ⊃**Music Row,** near downtown, offers two atmospheres. First, there's the touristy strip where the stars have their own museums and souvenir shops. Then there's the music-related businesses and studios located along a series of streets with such names as Music Circle and Music Square.

Barbara Mandrell Country anchors the activity along the strip on Demonbreun Street and features the star's memorabilia and a large gift shop. Other smaller museums and establishments of personal salutes in the area include the George Jones Car Museum, Hank Williams, Jr. Museum, and souvenir shops owned by and featuring items of Randy Travis, Conway Twitty, Willie Nelson, and many others.

For the person who wants to stay away from the souvenir shoppers, a stop at the **Country Music Hall of Fame** is a must. Located at 4 Music Square East, the museum covers the genre from the beginning. Run by a foundation, the facility offers a low-key alternative to the other hubbub along Music Row. A tour of RCA's Studio B complex, the site of early recordings by Elvis and other country icons, is also offered by the museum. Admission is charged; (615) 242–5167.

Songwriting is a revered occupation in Nashville. No other city pays attention to its writers the way Music City does, and radio announcers are just as apt to say who wrote a song as who performed it. "Writers' Nights" are held in various locations on a regular basis and are great places to get right down to the basics of country music. Hearing a popular writer singing his or her list of hits that others made into million-sellers is like listening to an oldies jukebox.

Perhaps the best-known cafe in the city, **The Bluebird** is also one of the best places to attend a writers' night. The food is good, the talent is excellent, and chances are good that you might be sitting next to a country superstar. They hang out here a lot, especially during writers' shows. Several of today's superstars were regulars here on their way up the ladder, including Garth Brooks and Kathy Mattea. The Bluebird is located in the Green Hills area of the city, about fifteen minutes from downtown at 4104 Hillsboro Pike; (615) 383–1461.

Just north of downtown, ⊃**The Museum of Tobacco Art and History** features a collection of cigar-store figures, a snuff box collection, tobacco-related memorabilia, advertising items, and a noted collection of Meerschaum pipes. A subsidiary of U. S. Tobacco, the museum offers free tours Monday through Saturday. It's located in that company's manufacturing plant at 800 Harrison Street; (615) 271–2349.

In the heart of downtown lies the **Tennessee State Capitol**. Finished in 1859, it was designed by William Strickland, who also helped design the U.S. Capitol. The beautiful building is being renovated in stages, and it is undervalued by tourists. Strickland loved the place so much that he requested to be interred in its walls. President James K. Polk is also buried there. Admission free; (615) 741–0830.

The Museum of Tobacco Art and History

Down the street from the Capitol is the **Arcade,** which is being restored to its finest. It was built in 1903 as a two-tiered shopping mall, an identical copy of one in Milan, Italy. Today, it is occupied by specialty shops, including the mandatory roasted-nut store, whose aroma pervades the entire complex.

Several decades before the city was known for its music, it had a reputation as a regional center of culture and education. Numerous colleges advanced the learning of the classics, and it wasn't long before the city was known as the Athens of the South. In 1896, it was only natural for planners of the state's centennial celebrations to elaborate on this classic theme.

An exact replica of the ⊃**Greek Parthenon,** with a tolerance of less than $1/_{16}$th of an inch, was built for the huge exposition, held in what is now known as Centennial Park, just a few miles out West End Avenue from downtown. The newly restored Parthenon now houses art exhibits and serves as a backdrop for various cultural events in the park. A 42-foot replica of *Athena Parthenos* is in the process of being sculpted. Admission is charged; (615) 862–8431.

For the best fried chicken and country ham dinners in Middle Tennessee, follow West End Avenue (it turns into Highway 100 farther out) to the **Loveless Motel and Cafe.** It's about 15 miles from downtown. Owner Donna McCabe has herself a neat piece of roadside Americana here, including a colorful neon sign. The food is served family style, with fresh biscuits and homemade preserves. While you're waiting for a table, be sure to read the clippings on the walls. This place has been visited by some very important people through the years, including Captain Kangaroo. It's located in a little house, so reservations are almost a must. Open daily from 8:00 A.M. to 2:00 P.M. and 5:00 to 9:00 P.M. Closed Mondays. (615) 646–9700.

If you're a beer can collector, the ⊃**Museum of Beverage Containers and Advertising** might very well be heaven for you. It's located about 16 miles north of Nashville in the small community of Goodlettsville. Their collection of 25,000 soda and beer cans is claimed to be the largest in the world. In addition, the museum has more than 5,000 antique soda bottles on display and a great display of advertising pieces used by various bottlers during the years. Admission is charged; (615) 859–5236.

The Parthenon, Nashville

Sumner County

Across the county line from Goodlettsville, north of Hendersonville, country music reigns as king. ⊃**Twitty City,** the home, office, and museum of entertainer Conway Twitty, offers a glimpse into the life-style of this rich and famous superstar. The nine-acre complex has live entertainment during the summer months and a gift shop and food concessions area.

The organized tour takes you through an air-conditioned showcase that features Twitty's life from birth to the present. In addition to his 50-some gold records, more than won by Elvis or the Beatles, you'll get an opportunity to see his lime-green, 1956 Thunderbird, which has only 61 miles on it. The tour also takes you through the gardens and the first floor of Conway's home.

From Thanksgiving through the first week of January, more than 500,000 lights and numerous holiday events keep the place hopping. Locals call the winter event "Twismas at Twitty City." Admission charge to parts of the complex; (615) 822–6650.

In Castalian Springs, what may be the largest log structure ever erected in Tennessee still stands. **Wynnewood** was built in 1828 as a stagecoach inn and mineral springs resort, and by 1840 a row of cottages adjoining the inn had been built, as well as a horse racetrack.

The main house is 142 feet long with a "dog-trot" through the middle. Some of the logs, mostly oak and walnut, are 32 feet long. All the rooms have outside doors and are entered from a gallery that extends 110 feet across the back of the building. A stairway in the dog-trot goes to the second-story rooms.

Owned by the state, Wynnewood is located 45 miles northeast of Nashville, 8 miles east of Gallatin on Highway 25. Open year-round, seven days a week. Closed Sundays from November 21 through April 1. Admission charged; (615) 452–5463.

About one hundred yards east of the entrance to Wynnewood is a stone monument marking the location of a giant, 9-foot-diameter sycamore tree in which Thomas Sharp Spencer lived during the winter of 1778–79. Spencer, the first white settler in middle Tennessee, called the tree home while he was building a cabin nearby.

Also located along Highway 25, about 5 miles from Gallatin, is Cragfront, one of the finest examples of Federal architecture in the state. Built between 1798 and 1802 by General James Winchester of Revolutionary War fame, the house has been restored and is open to the public. Open mid-April through October, daily except Monday. Admission charge; (615) 452–7070.

Wilson County

Randy Carpenter enjoys walking among his buffalo herd, but he doesn't recommend it for his guests. "People have to remember these are wild, exotic animals, and they can turn on you pretty quick," he said.

You'll find anywhere from 50 to 200 animals on Randy's 185-acre **Buffalo Farm.** He breeds and raises them, and then sells them to others who want to do the same. Many end up on people's dinner plates. A three-ounce piece of buffalo meat has 1.3 grams of fat and 93 calories compared to 8.7 grams of fat and 183 calories for beef. Beefalo meat falls in the middle range. As the health aspects become wider known, Randy's buffaloes are more in demand.

Visitors are welcome, but Randy cautions people not to go wandering out in the fields. He has a sign (in the shape of a buffalo) posted that tells visitors not to attempt to cross the field unless they can do it in 9.9 seconds, because the buffalo can do it in ten seconds. Actually, the animals can run 35 miles an hour and can jump 7 feet straight up from a standing position.

Take Old Hartsville Highway out of Lebanon and go 9.9 miles. Turn right on Speck Road and go 1.5 miles. Take a right on Mitchell Road; the farm is down about 1.5 miles. The buffalo range in a field that has about a mile frontage on Mitchell Road, and you can get a good glimpse of the animals there. But if you'd like to talk with Randy and see the rest of his operation, call first and he'll be happy to show you around. (615) 444–8568.

Williamson County

The country stars and the top bankers and businesspeople of the state might make their millions in Nashville, but when it comes to investing in their life-styles and families, many come south to this county. It consistently has the state's highest per capita income and the lowest unemployment rate.

Maps that show where many of the stars live are available at most bookstores. Dolly Parton, Gary Morris, The Judds, Tom T. Hall, Minnie Pearl, and Waylon Jennings are among the inhabitants of the area. If you want to see them, you probably have a better chance hanging out at the local Kroger store than in front of their houses.

Franklin, the county seat, is 17 miles south of Nashville and is associated with old, restored homes and businesses, antique shopping, and the Civil War. The entire downtown section is on the National Register of Historic Places.

The ⊃**Carter House,** south of downtown on Columbia Avenue, was caught in the middle of the fight aptly known as the Battle of Franklin on November 30, 1864. Bullet holes are still evident in the main structure and various outbuildings. One of the outbuildings has 203 bullet holes in it, making it the most battle-damaged building from the Civil War still standing anywhere.

The property is one of the eleven historic sites in the state owned and operated by the Association for the Preservation of Tennessee Antiquities. Open daily; admission charged; (615) 791–1861.

Across the street is **The Bunganut Pig,** an English-style pub. Great food, drinks, and atmosphere. Children are more than welcome. (615) 794–4777.

About 5 miles away, the ⊃**Carnton Mansion** also played an important role in the Battle of Franklin. On the rear lines of the Confederate forces, the elegant estate witnessed a steady stream of dying and wounded during the battle. At one time, the bodies of five slain Confederate generals were laid out on the back porch. Within view of that historic porch rests the only privately owned Confederate cemetery in the United States. Open daily; admission charged to house; cemetery free; (615) 794–0903.

A few blocks east of the town square, where the Confederate monument (circa 1899) rests, is the **Hiram Masonic Lodge.** When the three-story building was built in 1823, it was said to be the tallest structure in Tennessee. It was constructed to house the first Masonic Lodge in the state, chartered in 1803, and later, in 1827, the first Protestant Episcopal Church in Tennessee was founded here.

The Catholic church next to the lodge was built in 1871 from bricks fired on the site. Today, the church owns land on both sides of the lodge and was virtually built around it.

Rutherford County

One mile from downtown Murfreesboro is an obelisk marking the geographic center of the state. "The Dimple of the Universe," as it is called locally, is on Old Lascassas Pike. Turn left off Greenland Drive opposite the football fields at Middle Tennessee State University.

Farther out Highway 96, just past Lascassas, lies the small unincorporated village of Milton. With a population of about 200, the place has two businesses, the mandatory post office and ⊃**Manuel's Cajun Country Store.** The latter is the place to be.

Among the grocery items, which include Louisiana specialties such as syrup, coffee, and hot sauces, are red-checked, oilcloth-covered tables that come alive four days a week with the best Cajun food in the state. Abe and Dottie Manuel head up the family operation while the rest of the family cooks and serves the fried alligator (in season), shrimp, crayfish, and other ethnic specialties. The Manuel relatives in Creole, Louisiana are involved. They trap the 'gators the restaurant serves.

On Friday nights, a Cajun band fills the streets of Milton with music as it plays from the front porch and people dance on Main Street. Meals are served from 11:00 A.M. to 5:00 P.M. Wednesdays and Thursdays, and from 11:00 A.M. to 9:30 P.M. on Fridays and Saturdays; (615) 273–2312.

One of the most interesting factory tours in the state is located north of Murfreesboro, just off Highway 41. The ⊃**Nissan Motors Manufacturing Corporation** Truck/Auto Plant offers tours on Tuesdays and Thursdays. During the forty-five-minute trek through the modern plant you'll see men and women working arm and arm with more than 230 robots to produce the 500 vehicles that the plant turns out each day.

You'll see some workers dipping parts into paint while others slam doors. The complex covers about 800 acres and employs a great many of the locals. To be safe, it's best to call ahead to see if they are planning on giving tours the day you want to be there. Admission is free, but of course they don't give samples. (615) 459–1444.

The life of Billy Lynch is centered on one single corner in the middle of Eagleville, population 460. He runs **Lynch's Restaurant and Dairy Bar,** and he's the mayor of the town.

The forty-year-old restaurant is located at the corner of Highway 41A and Highway 99. City Hall is just a few steps across the parking lot from the diner. Although he's not sure if he'll run for mayor again when his term expires in 1994, he is sure he'll still be running his eatery. "I spend about 90 percent of my time on this corner, and I'm here to close the place just about every night," he said.

Between shifts at the restaurant, Billy takes his apron off and runs across to the city hall to see if anything needs his attention. Meanwhile, his thirty-two-seat diner keeps packing them in. Open 5:00 A.M. to 8:30 P.M. seven days a week, Lynch's is known for the "meat and three" plate lunches it serves every day. You get a meat dish and three vegetables for $3.00. On Fridays he buys up a mess of fresh catfish and offers a fish fry dinner for $4.95.

Dessert? With "Dairy Bar" as part of the name of the establishment, you can only imagine some of the delightful ice cream dishes Billy and his crew serve up. And that's not to mention the fresh-baked pies available each day!

Open every day except Thanksgiving and Christmas. (615) 274–6427.

Coffee County

If you happen to be in Manchester during the early part of October, be sure to visit the **Old Timer's Day** celebration. The city fathers shut down the streets around the square for a Saturday and fill it with fun things to do, including a bluegrass music concert, arts and crafts, kiddie rides and games, and a whole lot of food. (615) 728–7635.

On Highway 55, just before you reach Tullahoma, be on the lookout for the **Coca-Cola Bottling Company** plant. Next to it is the Company Store, a retail outlet open to the public. You'll be amazed at how many things are made with the Coke logo on them. It's a virtual plethora of Coke red and white merchandise, from clothes to antique reproductions to glasses. Open Monday through Saturday, 10:00 A.M. to 6:00 P.M.; (615) 454–1030.

In Tullahoma, at 2102 North Jackson Street, **Worth Inc.** operates the world's largest bat and ball manufacturing plant. The company makes more than seven million balls and more than a million bats each year. There's another company that makes more balls, and another that makes more bats, but none can top Worth for combined production.

Worth brand softballs include the Red Dot, Blue Dot, and Green Dot brands and the RIF (reduced injury factor) baseball. The patented RIF greatly reduces hit-by-baseball (and softball) injuries, and its sales are skyrocketing each year. In fact, Worth doesn't make a traditional youth baseball anymore.

The Tennessee Thumper is but one of the baseball bat brands Worth creates. It also custom-makes bats for more than sixty professional baseball players.

Tours are given on Wednesdays if they know you're coming. On your trek through the plant you'll see northern white ash being turned into bats on a lathe, and you'll get to talk with the women who hand sew all the baseballs and softballs. They'll show you how they do it, and they might give you a chance to work on one as well. You'll also walk through the stamping and boxing operation. (615) 455–0691.

It wasn't soft drinks that George Dickel of ↄ**George Dickel Distillery** had in mind when he and his wife arrived in Tullahoma in the 1860s. He was searching for the right water to make whiskey. He found the townsfolk sipping a limestone water from nearby Cascade Spring; he investigated, liked what he tasted, bought some land, and in the early 1870s opened his distillery.

The facility closed in 1911 when the state went dry but was reopened by Schenley Distillers in 1958 when the state voted to allow the manufacture of alcoholic products. Most of Coffee County remains dry to this day. The whiskey is still made the old-fashioned way, and all through the free tour, people are reminded that this is not bourbon but Tennessee sour mash whiskey. The difference is in the charcoal-mellowing processing.

Miss Annie runs the George Dickel General Store, located across the wooden bridge, which spans Cascade Creek. Ask her how you can be recognized for your good taste, and she'll hand you an application blank for the George Dickel Tennessee Whiskey Water Conservation Society. Head north on Route 41A from Highway 55 for about 5 miles and then turn right on Marbury Road and follow the signs. Tours are weekdays only. Admission free; (615) 857–3124.

Moore County

Deep in this dry county, you'll find another, possibly more famous, distillery known for its Tennessee sour mash whiskey. ⊃**Jack Daniel's Distillery** put Lynchburg, a community of 360 residents, on the map.

Mister Jack (as he is locally known) founded his business in 1866 and received the first federal license ever issued for a distillery. It still holds that number-one distinction.

If you want to take a tour, make sure you wear comfortable shoes: there's a lot of walking and hill climbing. This is true history and Americana at its finest. They'll even let you taste the sour mash by dipping your fingers into the vat during the tour, but since this is a dry county, no samples are permitted.

One of the highlights of the tour is the visit to Daniel's office, left virtually the way it was when he died. Make sure you ask the guide to show you where Mister Jack lost his temper one day, eventually causing him to experience a slow, painful death.

Free lemonade and coffee are available at the visitors center. Nothing is for sale here, but the employees will direct you into the village of Lynchburg to the bevy of shops there. If you're looking for a wide range of Jack Daniel's items as well as crafts and old-time items, the best place to visit is the Lynchburg Hardware, the Barrel Shop, or the Lynchburg Ladies Handiwork, all on the town square. Distillery tours are given daily 8:00 A.M. to 4:00 P.M. Closed Thanksgiving, Christmas, and New Year's Day. Free; (615) 759–4221.

Across the square, **Miss Mary Bobo's Boarding House** still dishes out the best meal in town. Miss Mary started her business in a pre-Civil War building in 1908 and served many a meal to Mister Jack and visiting VIPs. Of course, Miss Mary doesn't serve up the vittles these days—but the present owners do in true Bobo fashion. Because the seating capacity is only sixty-five, reservations are almost a must for the family-style meals. The local wags call it the Bobo Hilton. Lunch is the only meal served, and it's on the table promptly at 11:00 A.M. and again at 1:00 P.M. Adults pay $9.75 and have a choice of two meats, six vegetables, bread, beverage, and dessert. Kids eat for $5.00. (615) 759–7394.

Franklin County

As you head west across the mountain from Monteagle on Highway 41A/64, you'll pass the beautiful **University of the South** in Sewanee. Founded in the late 1850s, the 10,000-acre mountaintop campus is known for its shady lawns and Gothic sandstone buildings patterned after Oxford University in England.

Farther down the mountain you'll enter the village of Cowan, where you'll find the **Cowan Railroad Museum** along the still-busy railroad tracks. The museum is housed in the large circa-1904 depot that once served as the busy passenger station.

People would come from all over the south to visit the Sewanee area and the Monteagle Assembly. They would disembark from the passenger train in Cowan and take the "Mountain Goat," a smaller train, up the mountain to their destinations.

Today the museum is full of railroad antiques and memorabilia of those early days. Outside, there's a steam engine, a flat car, and a caboose. Run by volunteers, the facility is open from May through October on Thursdays, Fridays, and Saturdays from 10:00 A.M. to 4:00 P.M., and on Sundays from 1:00 to 4:00 P.M. (615) 967–7365.

The old Franklin County jail in Winchester had one of the nicest views that any prisoner could ever hope for. Located along

81

the banks of the Boiling Fork Creek, the structure, built in 1897, served as the county's penal institution for seventy-five years. When the new jail was built, the property was turned over to the county's historical society, which then turned it into the **Old Jail Museum.** In addition to the museum, the cell area and the maximum security cell block are retained as they were. (615) 967–0524.

Heading west on Route 64, you'll see one of the few large castles still left in America. ɔ**Hundred Oaks Castle** was built by Arthur Handley Marks, son of the state's twenty-first governor. Marks traveled extensively through Europe and decided on his return to the family farm that he would build a castle around the existing structure.

What he built here is not the finished castle he had in mind. He died in 1892 of typhoid fever at the age of 28. If there were any plans for the building, they were haphazard at best. Turrets, towers, arched windows, and rounded columns appear randomly along the 100-foot-long roofline, seemingly placed there on a whim.

"He wasn't an engineer; he was a country gentleman who wanted a castle," said Deborah Rains, the facility director. Unfortunately, the castle was hit by a disastrous fire early in 1991, and the insurance company won't permit the public to tour the building until restoration is made.

However, enough of the building is intact for it to keep its Historic Register listing, and you can still see a lot of what has been called "an architectural wonder" from the street. Rains said she's thinking seriously about promoting it as an architectural ruins site. (615) 967–0100.

When you leave the castle, continue west on Route 64 and head into Davy Crockett country. You'll be going by a roadside marker designating "Kentuck," the homestead that he left in 1812 to go off to the Creek War. He and his first wife, Polly, and their children settled near here when he came back from the war. She died in 1815 and is buried in an old cemetery overlooking nearby Bean's Creek.

If you want any further information on Davy Crockett's ties with this part of Tennessee, stop by ɔ**Falls Mill** near Belvidere and talk with owner Janie Lovett. In addition to her duties at the mill she owns with her husband, John, she's active in the local historical association and seems to know everyone in the area.

The Lovetts bought the mill in 1984 and have been busy restoring since. Built in 1873, the mill has operated as a cotton-spinning and wool-carding factory, a cotton gin, a woodworking shop, and a grist and flour mill through the years. Since 1970, it has also served as a sort of museum. But it wasn't until the Lovetts bought it that it started realizing its true potential.

Make sure you take a walk down to the river behind the mill to get a good view of the falls and the 32-foot overshot waterwheel, which is believed to be the largest still in operation in the country. Also, if the miller is working, ask him to show you how to tie the traditional miller's knot.

Grain is still ground and is available at the mill store, along with other local items. There's a weaving exhibit upstairs in the mill, and outside, the reconstruction of an 1836 log stagecoach inn that will eventually serve as a bed and breakfast continues. It will open in early 1994.

Currently, an 1895 log cabin has been moved here and reassembled and serves as a bed and breakfast for up to four persons. Rates for the cabin range from $48 to $53 per night for four people. The mill and picnic grounds are open daily. Admission is charged; (615) 469–7161.

Bedford County

Shelbyville, the county seat, is also the center of Tennessee's horse country. It plays host each year to the **Tennessee Walking Horse Celebration,** an event during which the World Grand Champion is named.

This special breed of horse, developed during 150 years of selective breeding, is promoted today as the "world's greatest show and pleasure horse." The horse has an unusual rhythmic gliding motion in which each hoof strikes the ground separately in an odd one-two-three-four beat.

The breed emerged from the plantations around here during the later part of the nineteenth century but today can be found across the country. The area around Shelbyville is still known for its farms, and most of the owners are happy to show off their facility. Many have signs out welcoming you, but you might want to call the Breeders Association in advance. There may be a special event or training session at one of the farms that you'd find interesting. (615) 359–1574.

While you're in Shelbyville, stop by **Pope's Restaurant** on the square for the best deep-fried chicken livers in the state. (615) 684–9901. Farther north on Highway 41A, business at ↄ**Carlton's General Store** in Rover is good. "Sure is—we sell something just about every day," claims owner Earl Carlton. "But the world is trying to crowd us out." (615) 294–5272.

Carlton, a character in his own right, has a small room next to his store where the locals come to solve all the world's problems. They start arriving about 5:30 A.M. and spend most of the day whittling and talking. "They whittle all the time and never make anything but a mess," complains Carlton, who is the seventh generation to live within a 2-mile area of the store.

Nobody seems to know exactly how Rover got its name, but the most accepted story is that a bunch of bickering regulars at a local drinking establishment decided to name their community. After hours of arguing over a name, one of them piped out, "Why don't we just call it Rover—we all fight like dogs anyway." So be it.

Along Route 269 in the northern corner of the county lies the quaint little village of ↄ**Bell Buckle.** The business district is chock-full of antique and craft stores and has one of the finest quilt stores in the state.

The village is also the home of **Webb School,** a preparatory school that has produced ten Rhodes Scholars and the governors of three states. The Junior Room, the original wood-shingled one-room schoolhouse built in 1870, has been preserved as it was then, complete with pot-bellied stove and teaching paraphernalia. It's open for visitors daily and is free. The school hosts a well-respected art and craft festival the third weekend of each October. (615) 389–6003.

ↄ**Wartrace,** down Route 269 a piece from Bell Buckle, also has a few antique shops, but its claim to fame is the world-famous **Walking Horse Hotel** and restaurant. The first world champion Tennessee walking horse, Strolling Jim, lived in the stables behind the hotel and is buried out under an oak tree. People are allowed to visit the stables, where a few walking horses live today, and the well-marked grave. Videos of the horses in action can be viewed in the hotel lobby.

The facility was built in 1917, a time when a great deal of its guests came by train. The tracks are still located within a stone's throw of the establishment's charming rocking chair–bedecked front porch.

Stop sign at Walking Horse Hotel, Wartrace

The hotel has twenty-five guest rooms, and to enter one is truly a step back in time. There are few, if any, modern frills in this hotel. It is being restored, room by room, without altering any of the hotel's old-time atmosphere. Room rates range from $33 to $43, with suites going for $57. (615) 389–6407.

Marshall County

For a reason no one can really explain, this area of the state is a haven for pencil manufacturing. Lewisburg's ⊃**Moon Pencil Company,** the nation's fourth-largest pencil company, is the only one that offers tours of its plant. Founded in 1961, the company specializes in non-yellow, specialized pencils that more often than not are sold to advertising-specialty companies that imprint various messages and logos on them and resell them.

On the tour, you'll get a close-up look at how the pencil, the one item you've probably used since childhood, is made. It's a four-step process, ending in the tipping (inserting erasers) and packing room.

Pencil producer Faber Castell is also located in Lewisburg, and Empire Pencil has its operation in nearby Shelbyville. Moon's plant manager, Doris Landtroop, is the official tour guide. (615) 359–1501.

Lawrence County

Although his legacy is divided among several areas in the state, David (a.k.a. Davy) Crockett only helped in the organization of one of the counties in which he lived, Lawrence County. He was working as a justice of the peace in the area in 1817 when it was ceded by the Chickasaw Indians to the United States. He helped get things organized and was instrumental in getting Lawrenceburg named as the county seat of government.

In 1922, during the dedication of a large monument that still stands on the south side of the square in Lawrenceburg, officials gave Crockett the title of "Father of Lawrence County."

By the way, the county was named in honor of Captain James Lawrence, who commanded a ship in the War of 1812. Mortally wounded, it was he who shouted out the famous command "Don't Give Up the Ship."

Wayne County

Up in the corner of the county, along the Tennessee River, is Clifton, the site of one of the last two ferry routes in western Tennessee. (The other is the Saltillo Ferry in Hardin County, 14 river miles upstream.) Here, Route 114 North is interrupted by a short ferry ride, then continues on into Decatur County on the west side of the river. The ferry operates seven days a week,

6:00 A.M. to 6:00 P.M. Operated by the state transportation department, the fee for a crossing is $1.00 per car.

Across Route 128 from the ferry landing is the longtime home of the great American novelist Thomas Stribling (1881–1965). He was born in Clifton and wrote many of his novels while residing in this house. One of his novels, *The Store,* won a Pulitzer prize in 1933. Plans are to turn the home, now owned by the city, into the **Stribling House Museum.**

Less than a mile out of town on Route 114, heading toward Highway 64, you'll find the **Clifton Motel,** owned by Tony Brown. In a room off the lobby, Tony has on display to the public his large collection of Indian artifacts. He has also assembled a nice collection of photos and memorabilia of early Clifton. There's no charge to peruse Tony's museum, and he'll be happy to point out a few of his personal favorites to you. (615) 676–3632.

Lewis County

The Natchez Trace is truly a road trip back in time. The 450-mile road has been a major highway between Nashville and Natchez, Mississippi, since the late 1700s. It is preserved today as a scenic two-lane parkway with few intersections, no commercial activities of any kind, and numerous pull-offs at historic stands (resting areas usually placed one day's travel from the other). The parkway, completed to Tennessee Highway 96W, 10 miles west of Franklin in Williamson County, will eventually extend to Nashville; its entrance will sit across from the Loveless Motel and Cafe on Route 100.

One of the early travelers on the trace was Meriwether Lewis, the famed leader of the Lewis and Clark expedition. In 1809 he met a violent and mysterious death at Grinder's Stand. His grave is marked by a broken column, symbolic of his broken career. The monument is located near the intersection with Tennessee Highway 20.

The trace is overlooked by those in a hurry because the 50 MPH speed limit is monitored quite closely. Make sure you have a lot of gas before you set out. For a map and other details, call (615) 796–2921.

The ↄ**Village of Hohenwald** is a junker's paradise. The downtown streets are lined with junk and secondhand clothing shops, and people come from miles away to do their bargain hunting. Used clothing is brought in from the Midwest and Northeast in bales and dumped on the floors of the shops. The bales are broken open each Wednesday, Saturday, and Sunday, the days to be there for the best selection. If you're knowledgeable about brands and clothing quality, some real big bargains await you here. There are tales about people finding money and even diamond rings in the old clothes.

German immigrants created Hohenwald (which means "high forest") in 1878 as they developed a lumber industry in the area. With the help of the railroad, an organized colony of Swiss immigrants settled in 1894 and built New Switzerland, just south of Hohenwald, and the two towns later merged. A great deal of the German architecture is still evident throughout the community.

The **Lewis County Museum of Natural and Local History,** located at 108 East Main Street, houses one of the largest collections of exotic animal mounts in the United States, including one example of each species of North American Sheep. There are also skins of lions, Bengal tigers, and tundra grizzlies. The museum serves as the local history museum and has several displays on the county's past. Open Wednesday through Saturday 10:00 A.M. to 4:00 P.M., and on Sunday 1:00 to 4:00 P.M. Admission charged.

If it's cement lawn items you're looking for, Randy Willis probably can help you out. Located 2 miles north of Hohenwald on Highway 48, Willis owns the **Willis Furniture Company,** which also manufactures and sells around 200 different ornamental cement art items for your yard. One of the best sellers recently has been a 3-foot-long green alligator on an aqua-colored base. Just the item to make your pool guests do a double take!

He'll be glad to show you around. (615) 796–4517.

Hickman County

There's not a single traffic light in the entire 613 square miles of this county. "We used to have one, but some kid kept shooting it out, and they finally took it down," said one county resident. While many of the communities in the state have groups who sit around outside near the courthouse and spit and whittle their days away, you'll find the old-timers in Centerville, the county seat in this county, playing checkers while they spit.

Nicknamed the Keg County, there's still a lot of moonshine made in these hills. If you're interested in sampling some, just put out the word. It has a way of finding you.

And speaking of tasty things, make sure you stop by **Breece's Cafe,** on the square in Centerville. In business since the 1940s, it offers country cooking at its finest. A different plate lunch is offered each weekday, and they always have a selection of home-baked pies on hand. Ask for the blackberry; it's especially good. Open Monday through Saturday 5:00 A.M. to 8:00 P.M., and Sunday 6:00 A.M. to 8:00 P.M. (615) 729–3481.

The strangest name of any community in the state is probably located here in Hickman County. Out on Highway 50, south of Centerville, is the small community of **Who'd A Thought It.** Story goes that a schoolhouse was being built out in the middle of nowhere, and a man pulls up in his buggy and asks what they were building. They told him, and he was last seen shaking his head and mumbling "Who'd a thought it" as he pulled away.

Other interesting names in the county are Defeated Creek, Little Lot, Only, Pretty Creek, Ugly Creek, Spot, and Grinders Switch. The Chamber of Commerce in Centerville has a book for sale that explains how more than sixty-four communities got their names, and where to find each. On the square; (615) 729–5774.

Up in Nunnelly, behind the Church of Christ where Highways 48 and 230 split, you'll find a monument marking the birthplace of Beth Slater Whitson, the writer of poems, songs, and short stories. Her best-known song lyrics were "Let Me Call You Sweetheart" and "Meet Me Tonight in Dreamland." She lived here from her birth in 1879 to 1913, when she moved to Nashville. She died there in 1930.

In the small community of Brushy, about halfway between Hohenwald and Centerville on Highway 48, you'll find a prime example of preserved southern culture. Discount stores, supermarkets, and large auto services, which have collectively closed down a lot of mom and pop operations, have not been able to put Robert and Sharon Rogers out of business. The two own the **Brushy Store and Cafe.** Inside you'll be able to buy a can of Spam or a tube of toothpaste or have your chain saw sharpened. But if you look beyond all those crackers, you'll see the real ritz to this operation . . . the cafe.

Sharon does the cooking and baking in this "meat and three" eatery. Specializing in southern plate lunches, she offers a meat (different each day), three vegetables, and homemade biscuits or bread for $3.25. Chicken and dumplings are a favorite of her regulars, as are her cobbler and fruit pies.

Special orders? Sure, why not. Call ahead and tell her what you want, and she'll do her darndest to have it ready for you when you show up. That's the advantage of having a restaurant in a grocery store. Open from 7:00 A.M. to 5:00 P.M., six days a week; (615) 729–3805.

Humphreys County

The coal miner's daughter not only lives in Hurricane Mills, she owns it. When country music's most-awarded female vocalist, Loretta Lynn, and her husband, Mooney, were house shopping back in 1967, she was searching for a big old "haunted looking" place. When she saw this century-old mansion, she knew this was her dream. She wanted it immediately, not knowing the entire town and old mill came with it. The ꓷ**Loretta Lynn Ranch,** on Route 13 in Hurricane Mills, is her home as well as her museum and special place to welcome fans.

In 1975 a campground was developed, and since then numerous other attractions have been added to the ranch, including Loretta's personal museum, a replica of the coal mine her father worked in, a replica of her "Butcher Holler House," a Western store, and a gift shop.

Tours of the first floor of her antebellum plantation mansion are given daily. Make sure you ask the guide about the haunted aspects of the building. There is no charge to enter the ranch, but there is for the tours, museum, and other activities, including miniature golf and canoeing. There are dances every Saturday night during the summer, and Loretta schedules a few concerts during that time also. When she's home, she enjoys walking around meeting people and signing autographs. Open April through October. (615) 296–7700.

A few miles north on Route 13, Hunter Pilkinton lives out his fantasy in his ꓷ**World O'Tools.** "Everybody needs a world of something," said the lifelong collector. "Mine happens to be tools." Hunter's world contains more than 20,000 tools of all sorts and a large library of books and pamphlets about those tools. The museum is the result of a hobby that got out of control. A large building on the property contains his treasures.

The retired, personable Hunter has a story for each one of the items, and he'll tell you each one. It's best if you call first. "I may be out hunting for more tools and miss you." (615) 296–3218.

Along the Tennessee River at Highway 70 is the Johnsonville Tennessee Valley Authority (TVA) facility. Built in 1950, it was the TVA's first major coal-fired power plant. Tours are given "when someone shows up who wants one." The length of tour and how long you might have to wait for one to start can vary depending on the work load of the staff at that particular time. It's most likely they'll find time for you Monday through Friday during the morning or on Saturday morning, up until noon.

One of the things to look for during the tour is the coal-unloading facilities. If you're lucky enough to be there on the day the coal is being unloaded from a barge, you'll see a huge crane in operation that is capable of unloading coal at a net rate of 700 tons an hour. The coal then goes by conveyer to the crusher building, which is a sight in itself. After you leave here, you'll have a real appreciation for electricity and the work that goes into producing it. (615) 535–2561.

Dickson County

Charlotte, the seat of Dickson County, looks much as it did in the mid-1800s. The circa-1834 courthouse is still in use and is considered the oldest such building still in use in the state. Pre–Civil War buildings line the downtown square, and the old-timers still gather at the drug store on the square to solve the world's problems.

But it could have been so different! The now-quaint and quiet town was two votes short of becoming the capital of Tennessee. Only Nashville received more votes.

On the west square, the circa-1800 building in which **Old Bank Antiques** is located has been used as a tavern, a bank, and a private home. Today the store offers a full line of antiques and is open daily except Thursday, 10:00 A.M. to 5:00 P.M. Open Sunday by chance or appointment. (615) 789–5304.

North of Charlotte, just off Highway 48, you'll find Norman

Bowlby's collection of birds and goats. At any one time he has nearly one-hundred birds, including four different species of peacocks along with parakeets, turkeys, geese, and several species of ducks and chickens. You'll also find a few turkens, a half-chicken, half-turkey creation, walking around. "It's a hobby; I love exotic things," Bowlby said.

Five acres (including a small pond) of his 100-acre farm are dedicated to his birds and the goats. "The goats are a great clean-up crew," he noted. He loves company and is eager to show the birds to visitors. He's in the feeder pig business and usually has a lot of baby pigs that he'll also be glad to show you. Call him first and let him know you're coming. (615) 789–5536.

To find **Bowlby's nature park,** turn west on Harper Lane off Highway 48, just south of the BP service station. Then take a left on Old Highway 48 and go less than a half-mile to Daniel Lane. Take a right, and Bowlby Lane is on your right a half-mile down the road. The animals are located in pens at the front of the property.

When you leave the birds, go back out to Highway 48, take a left, and follow it to Dry Hollow Road, a couple miles up the road from the Bowlby spread. Take another left, and you'll enter the historic town of **Cumberland Furnace,** where an iron plantation village and iron furnaces thrived for nearly 150 years.

Today the area has more than thirty extant buildings related to the iron industry, and in 1988 the village was placed on the National Register as an Historic District. One of the owners of the iron business, Montgomery Bell, who bought the business in 1804, was the chief supplier of cannon shot to General Andrew Jackson's southern army in the War of 1812.

In 1891 the **Louisville and Nashville Railroad** built a branch line through the county with a spur to the village to serve the furnaces. The depot for that spur still stands today and is owned by Leslie Travis. The original, circa-1891 building was destroyed by fire in 1919 when a load of hot slag fell on it. The one standing today was built in 1920.

If Leslie is around, he'll be happy to talk with you about the area and to show off a couple of prized possessions he found in the woods near the old furnaces. One is a small cannonball; the other is a bar of pig iron, the kind that was shipped out of here to the manufacturing plants.

Next to the depot is the big red commissary building. Built in 1870, it was moved to the present location in 1906 and served as a company store until the mid-1920s. For more information, and for a detailed brochure of the history and a driving tour of the area, call the historic village association. (615) 441–1489.

Stewart County

The 170,000-acre peninsula between Kentucky Lake and Lake Barkley is owned and operated by the Tennessee Valley Authority and is aptly called the ⊃**Land Between the Lakes,** or LBL, as locals refer to it. About a third of it lies in Tennessee and the rest in Kentucky.

The area is an awesome display of nature. The Trace, the main north-south road, is 60 miles long, with southern entry just west of Dover, off Route 79. There's plenty to do here, and according to the rangers, most of the area is underutilized.

In addition to all the hiking trails and water activities, there are more than 100 miles of paved roads for biking. The **Homeplace** is a nineteenth-century living-history museum with sixteen restored structures that were moved from other LBL locations and rebuilt. Costumed personnel work the farm, and most will take time from their chores to talk history with you.

Homeplace employees eat here, with all food prepared over the open fires and in the kitchens of the restored buildings. While walking through the kitchens, talk with the cooks. They have some great stories to tell about their past cooking experiences.

Across the trace from the Homeplace, the largest federally owned herd of buffalo east of the Mississippi River roams the range. Here, the range consists of two 100-acre fields that hold up to fifty head of buffalo. Each animal needs about four acres to live and eat.

Although the American buffalo is associated with the western plains, herds ranged the Tennessee hills as well. In fact, many of the roads and highways in the state today follow old buffalo trails. If you want to see the herd, make sure you get there early in the morning. They have a tendency to disappear into the woods as the heat of the day increases.

There is a fee for many of the attractions, but to view the buffalo or hike the trails there is no charge. There are several special events during the year that the LBL newsletter covers in detail. Call for a free copy; (502) 924–5602.

Dover's Town and Country Restaurant, specializing in southern cooking, is a favorite among the locals for a good meal. You can order from the menu or partake of their breakfast, lunch, or dinner buffet. A special seafood buffet is offered on Friday and Saturday nights. Reservations are suggested for Saturday, especially during the summer. Open seven days a week from 5:00 A.M. to 10:00 P.M.; (615) 232–6930.

Montgomery County

Although it has to share honors with Kentucky, Montgomery County is the home of the famed 101st Airborne Division–Air Assault of the U.S. Army. The Fort Campbell Military Reservation covers more than 100,000 acres on the state line and is the county's largest employer.

The base is open, which means visitors are welcome as long as they pick up a pass at Gate 4 on Highway 41A. Located near the gate is the visitors center and the Don F. Pratt Memorial Museum. Named after Brigadier General Don Pratt, who was killed while leading the 101st Airborne's legendary glider assault into Normandy, the museum traces the history of the division from World War I through the present. Exhibits also depict the history of Fort Campbell and the land it occupies.

Probably the most interesting exhibit in the place is the replica of the fragile-looking glider that the members of the 101st Division used in France during the D-Day invasion of 1944. More than 14,000 of the canvas-covered cargo gliders were built during the war, with such unlikely businesses as the Steinway Piano and Heinz Pickle companies contributing to the effort.

Across the street from the large indoor portion of the museum is a lot with a large collection of tanks, artillery field pieces, and airplanes. Open every day, 9:30 A.M. to 4:30 P.M.; admission free; (502) 798–3215.

Clarksville is the state's fifth-largest city, with a population of about 60,000, but it probably has the largest selection of architectural marvels of any one city in the state. "Anyone interested in architecture will have a field day in Clarksville," maintains the curator of the ⊃**Clarksville-Montgomery County Historical Society.**

Any tour through the city should start at the historical society's headquarters at the corner of Commerce and Second streets. Originally constructed as a U.S. Post Office and Customs House in 1898, its eclectic architecture consists of Italianate ornamentation, Far East-influenced slate roof, Romanesque arches, and Gothic copper eagles perched at each of the four corners.

Exhibits inside include one on the local tobacco industry and a salute to the local firefighters. This is one of the finest local museums in the state. Area tour maps can be picked up here. Open Tuesday through Sunday with the first Sunday of every month being "Free Sunday," when admission is free from 1:00 to 4:00 P.M.; admission is charged; (615) 648-5780.

There are two self-guided tours of the city and county—a 2-mile (twenty-five site) walking tour of the downtown architectural area and a 14-mile (fifty site) driving tour. One of the highlights of the walking tour is the Madison Street Methodist Church. Built in 1829 by a Jewish architect, the Star of David appears in the construction in at least two locations. Presumably they weren't discovered until after the architect got paid.

Mildred and Henry Plummer have had a great time running their little store for the past thirty-some years. ⊃**Plummer's Old Store and Museum,** located a few miles out of Clarksville on Highway 76 East, reflects that three-decade relationship. The seventy-five-year-old clapboard building, with berry bushes partially hiding the signs on the sides, does one of two things to a passing motorist. It either beckons him in or scares him away. And the latter would be quite a shame.

The Plummers are hospitable people who have lived next to their store for all but two years of its existence. Between the two structures, vegetable plants, fruit trees, and purple martin houses can be found.

Henry enjoys a good joke as well as anyone, and Mildred says people come just to hear his stories and to be had by his practical jokes. One corner of the store is set aside for "fun and silly" items. A large flat rock lies on the counter with the painted words, "Please turn me over." When you do, the painted message reads, "Thank you, that's much better."

Possibly the biggest draw is the museum. Henry estimates he has more than 1,000 items in the back of the store, separated from the rest of the establishment by chicken wire. A sign on the door explains what's back there. "Pre-electric and plastic, Granny's things, and Granpa's tools."

You'll never see a more eclectic collection in your life—from cherry pitters to slave shackles and chains to a chicken-head cutter. Henry is more than eager to walk you through and explain each item. Most of the stuff was given to him by people who knew he would take care of it for them. The Plummers are what true southern hospitality is all about. There's a small admission fee for the museum. (615) 358–9679.

Montgomery County's answer to California's Napa Valley can be found at the Beachaven Vineyards & Winery, a few miles off I-24's Exit 4. Co-owner Ed Cooke thinks his winery can offer as good a tasting tour as his counterparts in California. "We offer the same thing, but we add southern hospitality," he said.

Beachaven's tasting concept is a great plus for those needing a little education before buying a wine. Ed or one of the employees will be glad to give you a taste of all their varieties. Tours are given year-round for those who would like to see how the fruit of the vine becomes so divine. And these wines are really divine. Wine judges across the country think so too. Look at all those ribbons lining the walls awarded to the various products of Ed and his family. Their champagne is of "world renown," having been written up in the major wine books.

The most exciting (and aromatic) time to visit is in the fall while the crushing is taking place, but there is always something going on. During the summer, special concerts are presented in the vineyard's picnic area. They can't sell by the glass, but they would be glad to sell you a chilled bottle to enjoy with your cheese during a concert. (615) 645–8867.

Just outside Clarksville, the **Dunbar Cave State Natural Area** is 110 scenic acres of true history and legends. The activities on this site range from when the local Indians inhabited the cave entrance 10,000 years ago to when country music legend and Grand Ole Opry star Roy Acuff owned the property and held weekly country music shows in the cave entrance.

A stately old bathhouse now serves as a visitors center and museum. If you want to take a cave tour, you have to call ahead and see when the group tours are being held. Even if you don't take the tour, the museum and the nature trails make this a fun place to visit. Fishing is permitted on the lake. Located on Dunbar Cave Road, just off Highway 79, between Clarksville and I–24 (Exit 4). (615) 648–5526.

Robertson County

There have been ghosts and there have been legends, but the Bell Witch of ᗡ**Adams** is probably the most documented story of the supernatural in all of American history. This witch is unique because of the large number of people who have had direct experience with it.

John Bell was a well-respected and influential member of the Adams community. He and his family lived on a thousand-acre plantation along the Red River. The trouble started in 1817 when bumping and scratching sounds were first noticed, but the Bells passed them off as being caused by the wind. The big problems started in 1818, when continuous gnawing sounds were heard on each member of the family's bedposts each night. When someone would get up to investigate, it would stop. The sound would go from room to room until everyone was awake. Then it would stop until the candles were blown out and everyone went back to bed, when it would start all over again.

Things grew from there. People came to town to witness the occurrences and weren't disappointed. General Andrew Jackson came up to Adams from his Nashville home to investigate the matter but turned around when the wheels on his carriage mysteriously locked.

This has gone on through the decades. A few years ago, several reporters came to Adams with plans to stay in the Bell cave, where many of the experiences have occurred. They lasted a few hours before fleeing.

Today, the cave is sporadically open to the public for tours. All the Bell buildings are gone now, except for a small, log slave building. It has been moved to the grounds of the old elementary schoolhouse and is open for viewing. You can't miss the graves of the Bell family at the Bellwood cemetery. There's a magnificent tower marking the graves and a stone fence keeping the Bell Witch out.

The best place to start your tour of Adams is at the old school that is now known as the **Bell Witch Village Antique Mall,** run by Nina Seeley. She was a neighbor of Elvis Presley in Memphis but convinced her husband to move to Adams after reading about the witch. She's quite the promoter of the Bell Witch legend.

She and her late husband, Kenneth, were founders of the Bell Witch Opry. For the past sixteen years, the Opry has been held each Saturday night at 7:30. It's a country music show featuring Nina, as well as some up-and-comers who just might show up on the Grand Ole Opry in the next few years. The show is held upstairs in the old schoolhouse. Admission is $3.00 per person, one of the best entertainment values in this neck of the woods. (615) 696–2762.

The **Tennessee-Kentucky Threshermen's Association** holds its annual wheat threshing and steam engine show at the school during the last part of July. Antique threshers, tractors, and hundreds of other steam engines are in action during the event. There are also an arts and crafts show, a quilt show, and live musical performances. (615) 696–2058.

If you've ever wondered where those wild horses and burros that are rounded up from the western wilds go, you need not wonder anymore. Many of them come to Cross Plains and are adopted out of the ⊃**Southeastern Wild Horse and Burro Adoption Center.** On any given day, the pens are full of animals from Nevada, Arizona, New Mexico, and California waiting for new homes.

The adoption program is a partial solution to the problems of overpopulation among wild horse and burro herds that roam public rangelands in ten western states. When this facility opened in 1979, it was the East's first waystation for these animals. Due to budget cuts it is now the last center in the East. The center is run by Randall and Paula Carr on their 200-acre farm and is funded by the federal government.

Each year during the last weekend in August, the center holds the **Tennessee Wild Horse & Burro Days** celebration and invites those who have adopted to bring back the animals and compete in the Middle Tennessee Mustang Association Horse Show. The adoption center is off Highway 25, just outside the village of Cross Plains. There's no charge unless you take a horse or burro home with you. In that case, it'll cost you up to $125. Open year-round, Friday through Sunday; (615) 654–2180.

Cheatham County

While new 1950s-style eateries currently are being built across the country, **Stratton's Restaurant and Soda Shop,** in Ashland City, continues quietly to serve up ice cream and hamburgers as it has since 1954. The interior of this neat little place is truly a blast from the past.

"Everything you see in here is authentic, I guarantee it," said Steve Stratton, the founder's son and the current owner. From a 1954 Seeburg jukebox to original Coca-Cola posters on the wall, Stratton takes great pride in preserving the past in his popular establishment.

Built by his father in 1954 as the Dairy Dip, Steve has been running it since 1972. Originally primarily a carry-out that sat twelve people inside, Steve remodeled in 1985, expanding the eat-in capacity to fifty.

Traditional platters are served with house-made coleslaw or hush puppies. Besides the tasty burgers, menu items also include grilled chicken sandwiches, chopped steak, and char-broiled chicken breast.

But save room for dessert! Twenty-ounce malts are made with Carnation powdered malt, and other tasty concoctions can be made from soft-serve or hand-dipped ice cream. They also make their own fried pies.

You'll find Steve here every day except Sunday. Make sure you say hi to him; he'll be happy to share some of the history of the place with you. Located at 201 South Main Street; open 361 days a year; (615) 792–9177.

If it's a nice day, and you enjoy watching chain-saw artists, head out of town on Highway 49 West to the big bridge across the Cumberland River. Just before the bridge, on your left, you might see Michael Brumfield set up alongside the highway in front of a sawmill. This is his favorite weekend location. "If I feel like working outside, this is where I come," he said. If he's not there, give him a call and ask to see his famous cigar-store Indian works of art. (615) 792–7149.

Immediately on the other side of the bridge, take a quick left at the sign that claims this is the "home of the greatest catfish." The **Riverview Restaurant and Marina** are located down the hill along the river. In addition to a boat ramp and marina, the restaurant offers a great view of the river while you enjoy its fresh catfish.

99

Off the Beaten Path on the Western Plains

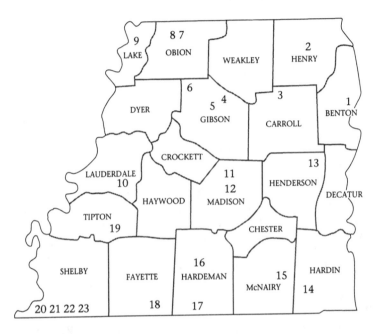

1. Tennessee River Folklife Center
2. Culpepper's Store
3. Tennessee's First Driver's License
4. Kingdom of Skullbonia
5. Doodle Soup Capital
6. White Squirrels
7. Obion County Museum
8. Dixie Gun Works
9. Reelfoot Lake
10. Alex Haley House Museum
11. Tennessee Woods Art Gallery
12. Casey Jones Home and Railroad Museum
13. World's Third Largest Pecan Tree
14. Shiloh National Military Park and Cemetery
15. Buford Pusser Home and Museum
16. Little Courthouse
17. Flying Feathers Quail Farm
18. LaGrange
19. Bozo's Restaurant
20. Graceland
21. Beale Street
22. Mud Island
23. Peabody Hotel

The Western Plains

Benton County

Nathan Bedford Forrest, the notorious hard-riding Confederate cavalry officer known for his unexpected and often offbeat tactics, pulled off one of the Civil War's most interesting victories along the Tennessee River here in the fall of 1864. It was probably the first time in military history that a calvary force attacked and defeated a naval force. High atop Pilot Knob, the highest point in this part of the state, Forrest secretly assembled his troops. He had his eye on the Union army's massive supply depot, directly across the river.

At the time, the depot had more than thirty vessels, most fully loaded, waiting to head out to Union forces. Stacks of supplies lined the wharf. Forrest attacked and caught the Yanks off guard. Within minutes, all thirty vessels and the various warehouse buildings were on fire, and within two hours everything was destroyed. By nightfall, Forrest's troops had vanished into the dense woods.

The land surrounding Pilot Knob is now known as the **Nathan Bedford Forrest State Park.** Atop the hill is a monument to Forrest. Also at the top is the つ**Tennessee River Folklife Center,** "designed to explore the relationship between the river and the people who use it."

Most of the exhibits incorporate segments of oral histories taken from the locals who "lived the life." Separate accounts recall the early industries, and the music, religion, and community events of the area.

The most colorful audio presentation highlights the days when folks would gather at the river to welcome the big showboats to their landing. The biggest exhibit is "Old Betsy," an entire workboat from the early musseling industry along the river. The most visual representation of early river life is from the Brownie camera of Maggie Sayre. She lived on a houseboat for more than fifty years and photographed everyday life around her.

Most rural areas throughout the South have their own version of the liar's bench and the spit and whittle club. The view from the porch or from under the tree may be different from town to town, but the plot is the same. A story is told, then retold, then exaggerated to the point where it becomes a modern-day myth. A typical riverfront liar's bench has been reconstructed here at the center, with a breathtaking view of the Tennessee River far below. Walk up, push a button, and sit down and relax. The series of taped stories (from original spit and whittlers) will keep you in stitches.

The center is open daily. Admission free; (901) 584–6356. The historical park area offers camping, hiking trails, and picnic areas. Both areas are located at the end of Highway 191, about 10 miles out of Camden.

John Latendresse has developed his own techniques for developing freshwater pearls in mollusks taken from the nearby Tennessee River. He is regarded as the first person in America to culture pearls. From an idea in a lab in the early 1960s, his pearl venture has grown to include several companies and more than 120 employees. Much of the technique is still considered "secret" by Latendresse. The mussel is implanted with a nucleus, which then "grows" into a cultured gem, known as the Tennessee Pearl. The process takes from one to three years, depending on the type of mollusk used and the type of pearl being cultured.

Many of the pearls are used by **American Pearl Creations,** also owned by Latendresse, to make jewelry for its 3,000-plus clients. Because of the secret nature of the pearl culturing, tours of that end of the business are somewhat limited at particular times, but there's plenty to see in the jewelry-making end of things. (901) 584–8285.

Tennessee ranks twelfth in the nation in sorghum production, and Benton County is one of the largest producers in the state. Madison and Donice Furr run the **Tennessee Sorghum Company,** one of the largest operations in the county.

Sorghum is mainly used as a sweetener and is rich in vitamins. It's used in gingerbread and is poured over hot biscuits and butter. "It's very good and very healthy for you," claims Donice. "We sell a lot of it to health food stores."

The Furrs grow about thirty acres of sorghum cane and produce their own syrup. They also buy from other Benton County sorghum producers and market the product under the Tennessee Sorghum Company moniker. Locally produced honey is also available.

The most aromatic time to visit the Furrs' operation is in the fall when the sorghum cane is being stripped of its juices and cooked down to the right consistency. The cooking is done down at the Furrs' farm, and the marketing and packaging takes place at their warehouse in Camden.

Donice welcomes visitors to the farm and promises to let them "stick a finger" in the cooking sorghum for a once-in-a-lifetime taste treat. The farm is located off Highway 192, about 5 miles north of Holladay. Call her and see if anything is going on the day you want to go out, and she'll give you specific directions. (901) 584–3322.

Henry County

There's no place better than an organized wildlife refuge to observe that area's wildlife population, and the **Tennessee Wildlife Refuge** is no exception. Nature trails, paved roads, and observation points are plentiful in this 80-mile-long area along the Tennessee River. The area is an important resting and feeding place for migrating waterfowl each winter.

Beginning about mid-October, up to 100,000 Canada geese and 250,000 ducks start their annual fall trek to the refuge where they will spend the winter. The major attraction here for the animals is the farming program, which provides them with a great deal of food all winter long.

In addition to the waterfowl, the refuge is home for more than 200 species of birds, a fact that brings in serious bird watchers from all over the country. Maps, brochures, and specific wildlife information is available. Open daily, year-round; (901) 642–2091.

In nearby Paris, the **"World's Largest Fish Fry"** is held at the end of each April. Since the early 1950s, the city has hosted the event at the fairgrounds and has achieved a (well-deserved) reputation for the quality of its catfish dinners and the traditional Tennessee way of preparing them.

Each year more than 10,000 pounds of fish are cooked in black pots containing more than 250 gallons of vegetable oil. The four-day event also includes a rodeo, a carnival, a three-hour parade, and a fishing rodeo.

The fish fry, the hunting, the fishing, and the proximity to Nashville were but a few of the reasons that country singing superstar Hank Williams, Jr. chose this area for his Tennessee home and business offices.

For a good bologna or ham and cheese sandwich, or for a bucket of minnows, crickets, worms, or chicken livers, stop by ⊃**Culpepper's Store.** Owners Trenton and Rita Ward can usually be found there as can Baby, their poodle. "We call ourselves a country place inside the city limits," Rita said. The small store specializes in bait and fishing supplies, as well as food and drink for the fishermen. Rita, who was born in Germany, is a favorite among the returning servicemen at nearby Fort Campbell. "As soon as they get back from Germany, they come in and want to show me how much German they learned while they were over there. It's also fun for me to hear about their impressions of my country."

Look for the American flags flying just inside the city limits on Route 69A. Even if you don't need any bait, stop by; Rita and Trenton will tell you about the area and some of the people who live around here. Open every day. (901) 642–8230.

Down Highway 79 is the small city of Henry, which might be the only city in the state with its executive offices housed in a log cabin.

Carroll County

Gordon Browning's first driver's license is on display at the **Gordon Browning Museum,** in the old post office building in downtown McKenzie. What makes that license so special is that it is ⊃**Tennessee's First Driver's License.**

Browning got it because he happened to be governor of the state in 1938, when licenses were first required. In all, Browning served three terms as governor. He was also a U.S. congressman, a chancery court judge, and he served in both world wars, and by the looks of the quantity of the memorabilia on display, he never threw anything away. A flag that he brought back from World War I is on display, as are various other patriotic mementos.

The museum is a great small-town collection dedicated to the life of the county's favorite son. It gives a good perspective on the values that he and the curator of the museum deemed important.

Mary Ruth Debault is the curator for the county historical society and probably knows more about this man than any living soul. The museum is open every day except Wednesday from 9:00 A.M. to 5:00 P.M., Saturdays from noon to 3:00 P.M. Admission is free. The museum is at 166 N. Main Street; (901) 352–3510.

Gibson County

When bare-knuckled pugilism was popular and legal in America during the first half of the nineteenth century, one area of this county was well known for its unique version of prize fighting sans gloves.

Skullbone and the surrounding ⊃**"Kingdom of Skullbonia"** hosted a type of fighting that became known as skullboning. All bare-knuckled punches had to be delivered to the head. Hits below the collar were not permitted and considered fouls.

To "play," fighters would stand opposite each other and take turns trading blows. Each round lasted until one would fall to the ground. The match lasted until one was satisfied that he had had enough.

After bare-knuckled fighting became illegal in America and communities went "underground" for the excitement, matches in Skullbone continued to be held in the open. When adoption of standard rules for prizefighting occurred in 1866, non-gloved activities died out just about everywhere except Skullbone, where it continued well into the twentieth century.

Today, just about all that remains of Skullbone is the general store, built in 1848. It has been owned since 1964 by Landon and Ruby Hampton and is known locally as **Hampton's General Store,** widely as the Skullbone Store.

The busy little store serves what is left of the "kingdom." Yellowed newspaper clippings of the area's heyday hang on the wall. Outside, the building is quite a landmark. With a map of the Kingdom of Skullbonia painted on one side and various soft drink signs and paintings on the front, a stranger can't drive by without stopping to investigate.

Across the street, a stacked row of directional road and mileage signs point the way to worldly centers such as Singapore, 9,981 miles; Anchorage, 3,320 miles; and Shades Bridge, 1 mile.

In addition to the regular fares of a country store, the Hamptons sell souvenir T-shirts. Skullbone isn't on most maps, but the Hamptons are trying to get Tennessee's governor to put it on the official state map. It's located on Highway 105, about 3 miles from Bradford. Open every day; (901) 742–3179.

It's amazing that just 3 miles away from the skullbone capital of the world one can find the ⊃**Doodle Soup Capital** of that

Signpost, Skullbone

same world. In fact, Doodle Soup is so popular in these parts that a festival is held in its honor each September.

What is Doodle Soup? It's a cold-weather dish, not good during summer because of its spicy nature. It's actually more of a sauce or gravy than it is a real soup. One of the most popular methods of eating it is by pouring it over a plateful of cracker crumbs or home-made biscuits, and letting it soak in for a while before eating.

Here is one of the "official" recipes. Be forewarned: There has been a battle going on for years as to which of the myriad recipes floating around should be considered official.

Take a large broiler chicken. Melt butter and run chicken all over. Put in broiler pan, split side down; salt to taste. Put in oven at 375 degrees; let cook until brown and tender. Take chicken out of the drippings that were cooked out in the pan. Add eleven cups of water, one cup vinegar, plenty of hot peppers, three tablespoons of cornstarch so it won't be just like water and will stay on biscuits good. Let cook until it gets as hot as you want. Taste it along.

Although it's a local tradition, most locals haven't eaten it, saying it sounds too "greasy." One restaurant, Jer-E-Lane, is rumored to have it on the menu occasionally.

In **Trenton** at the municipal building you'll find the world's largest collection of eighteenth- and nineteenth-century night-light teapots *(veilleuses-théières)*. A New York doctor, originally from Trenton, was going to give his multimillion-dollar collection of 500 pieces to the Metropolitan Museum of Art in New York City, but his brother convinced him to give them to his hometown instead.

Originally displayed in the trophy cases at the local high school, the unique collection found a permanent home when a new city building was built. The teapots now line the walls of the city's chambers. If you get there during regular business hours, you're welcome to walk around and study this one-of-a-kind collection. If you happen to get there late, a sign on the front door directs you to the firehouse where a friendly fire-fighter will hand over the key to city hall on the promise that you'll lock up and return the key before you leave town. Admission free; (901) 855–2013.

Up Highway 45W from Trenton is Rutherford, where a former home of Davy Crockett is open to the public. David (as residents prefer him to be called) moved to the area in 1823. His original cabin, built 5 miles east of town along the Obion River, was dismantled and stored with the intent of rebuilding it at a later date near where his mother is buried. But before it could be rebuilt, some of the logs were used in fires by campers.

Some of the logs were saved, though, and are now a part of the reproduction of that original cabin. On display are tools, furniture, and utensils from the period, as are letters that Crockett wrote home during his years in congress.

The cabin is open from the end of May through Labor Day Weekend. It's located on the city's grammar school property, on Highway 45W. Admission is charged; (901) 665–7166 and (901) 665–7339.

Farther up Highway 45W you'll find an amazing colony of ⊃**White Squirrels,** one of only a few such colonies in the world. As you enter Kenton, a town of about 1,500 residents, you'll be greeted by a big sign proclaiming, "Kenton. Home of the White Squirrels." Although the exact number is hard to pinpoint, as most white squirrels look alike, the city's official stance is that about 200 of the critters live here. The squirrels are fed by just about everybody, and there's a $50 fine if you kill one.

A wildlife biologist explains that the animals are actually "albino gray squirrels who have survived for so long because the people have taken such good care of them." They have inbred for so long that the normally recessive albino trait has become predominant.

Exactly how the first such squirrels came to the area about 120 years ago is the subject of a great many speculations. The most common theory is that during the early 1870s a band of Gypsies spent the night on a local farm. The next morning, in appreciation of the farmer's kindness, the leader of the Gypsies presented two white squirrels to the farmer. Thus it began.

The best time to see the flock (bevy? herd?) of white squirrels is in the morning and evening when they are most apt to be scurrying from tree to tree. Stop by the city hall, which also informally serves as a white squirrel visitors information bureau.

Obion County

The ⊃**Obion County Museum** in Union City is the only regional history museum in this part of the state. All the other museums are specialized, so this is the place to go to get a good overview of what northwest Tennessee is all about.

County historian Rebel C. Forrester is the perfect guide as he walks you through the displays and explains little tidbits of history that only a county historian would know. A collection of "documentary" photos from 1915–23 gives a good visual feeling to the other exhibits. Among the items on permanent display are a Model-T Ford, Indian artifacts, and a horse-drawn hearse.

Adjacent to the museum is a two-room log cabin with exhibits. The museum is open Saturday and Sunday afternoons and is located at 1004 Edwards Street, directly behind the high school. Admission free; (901) 885–6774.

About a block from the museum at the end of Edwards Street is the first monument erected in honor of the unknown Confederate soldier. It was dedicated on October 21, 1869. Some of the twenty-nine buried died in training at Camp Brown, here in Union City.

Gun collectors worldwide probably already know about this city's ⊃**Dixie Gun Works,** while noncollectors across town may never have heard of it. Founded by Turner Kirkland in the early 1950s, the business is now considered the world's largest supplier of antique guns and parts. The firm sells about 80,000 guns a year, including antique reproductions.

At any given time, a walk through the Dixie Gun Works' showroom is like walking through an antique firearms museum, except that you can buy most of the guns you see here. Usually, more than 1,500 guns are on display. Kirkland's other passion, antique automobiles, is also in evidence. Adjacent to the gun showroom is an auto museum with more than thirty cars, including a 1908 Maxwell.

A small log cabin gunshop is a part of this attraction. Originally built in this area around 1850, the shop contains two rifling machines and more than 1,000 gun-making tools. The complex is located on the Highway 51S Union City By-Pass. Admission charged for museum; (901) 885–0561.

North of Union City on the Kentucky border lies the early railroad center known as **Fulton.** Today, the city of Fulton is in Kentucky, while South Fulton is in Tennessee, although there is barely a line of demarcation.

The thing that made this railroad center different from most is that the city had the largest one-floor ice plant in America. The early railroad refrigerated cars needed ice, and this place had plenty to offer. One of the first transported refrigerated items requiring stops at numerous ice houses was the banana.

It wasn't long before this small town was the redistribution center for 70 percent of all bananas brought into America. For more than six decades, the community held that distinction. Now, to revitalize that heritage, the communities hold the **International Banana Festival** each September.

The four-day event includes banana-eating contests, parades, and the making of the world's largest banana pudding. The 2,000-pound creation is made by the chamber of commerce and is the highlight of the parade as it cruises by in a special see-through plastic vat. At the end of the parade, the pudding is scooped into 10,000 individual containers and given away free to the crowds.

The ice house burned down several years ago, and the trains don't run through downtown anymore; but while there's not much left of the old Fultons today, the area still plays an important role in the railroad industry. Fulton Yards is a busy hub for the Illinois Central System. Everything going north or south on the system comes through the yards.

While most of the physical aspects of the heritage is gone, the library keeps the memories alive year-round with exhibits and information on this once-thriving tropical industry. (502) 472–2975.

The Jack Flippen family, all three generations of them, are actively involved in the family's **Flippens Hillbilly Barn** business, just outside Hornbeak, about 16 miles from Union City. Originally established as an orchard, various parts of their business have grown from circumstances.

The Hillbilly Barn still sells apples and peaches but is into much more. Several years ago, the Flippens started selling apple cider and individual fried fruit pies at the encouragement of a local festival promoter. They have been frying pies and making cider ever since.

Mrs. Flippen started frying hamburgers when an orchard worker forgot to bring his lunch one day and asked her to fix him something to eat. That good deed on Mrs. Flippen's part has turned into a full-service "country-cooking" restaurant which is open seven days a week; Monday through Thursday, 8:00 A.M. to 6:00 P.M.; Friday and Saturday from 8:00 A.M. to 9:00 P.M.; and

Sunday, from 12:30 to 8:00 P.M. A large patio built over the lake allows outdoor seating, and an outdoor entertainment stage offers various types of live music. The homemade jams and jellies are quite popular, but through it all, the apple and peach fried pies remain the major reason for much of the return business. More than twenty-seven varieties of apples and peaches are also available.

To find the establishment, head west out of Union City on Highway 22. Go 8 miles and turn off the highway onto Shaw-town Road, and go 8 miles to the barn. (901) 538–2933.

Lake County

About ten minutes west of the Hillbilly Barn is ↄ**Reelfoot Lake,** the result of a true quirk of nature. The worst earthquake ever measured in American history took place in this area in 1812. On February 7, the quake hit, and the lands of northwest Tennessee near the Mississippi River dropped as much as 20 feet.

For fifteen minutes the river's water flowed backward to fill this major void, which had been a swampy forestland. Now, the area is a 13,000-acre shallow lake, 6 to 8 feet in depth, with the remains of the forest just under the surface, which makes boating quite an adventure. The water is a dark green color, with visibility never more than a few inches. The area surrounding the lake is now a state park, and a journey through here is truly a trek into unspoiled nature. The combination of shaggy cypress trees, some of them centuries old, and water lilies is most unusual for this state.

Because of its uniqueness, the lake's boaters were forced to create a special type of boat for easy navigation. Known as a "stump jumper," the boat is pointed at both ends, has a flat bottom, and is powered by a one-cylinder lawnmower engine that is capable of operating in 6 inches of water.

Reelfoot Lake is also the winter home to more than 100 American bald eagles. The birds, with wingspans of 6 to 8 feet, come here from their northern summer homes to spend the winter in a warmer, ice-free environment. The park provides numerous eagle programs, including bus tours of the area during winter.

The park's museum offers the chance to experience an earthquake firsthand. The 1812 quake has been reproduced, to a lesser degree, and allows guests to feel and hear what took place during those fifteen minutes. You can also sit in a stump jumper, learn about its creators, the Calhoun family, see Indian artifacts, and read firsthand accounts of the creation of the lake. The museum is also the loading site for the lake's sight-seeing cruises.

The park has camping sites, a camp store, rental cabins, and hiking trails. Guided hiking trips are offered during the year. A resort inn and restaurant, both owned by the state, are built out over the lake among the cypress trees. The entrance to the park is located off Highway 21.

An annual calendar lists the best times, month by month, to see the various wildlife around the lake. A copy can be obtained by calling the ranger's office; (901) 253–7756. A three-day arts and crafts festival is held each October at the park.

Of the world's talented songwriters, **Carl Perkins** is among the few who can actually say they helped launch an entire era of music. In Memphis during 1955 a young entertainer named Elvis Presley recorded the Perkins-composed "Blue Suede Shoes" and created a whole new sound in the process.

Perkins was born just 2 miles from Reelfoot Lake, in Tiptonville. Today his childhood home, on Highway 78S, is a museum filled with memorabilia. If you want a tour of the place, contact his cousin, Hubert Perkins, who owns Perkins Tire & Service in town. Give him a call at the service station, and he'll send someone down with a key to let you in. (901) 253–7653.

Lauderdale County

Henning, the boyhood home of the late author Alex Haley, is a picturesque town of Victorian homes and turn-of-the-century storefronts. The town probably would have progressed quietly like many small towns had it not been for native son Haley.

His 1976 Pulitzer-prize-winning novel, *Roots,* and the subsequent TV miniseries, based on the family stories his grandmother and aunt told him, brought international fame to Henning, where Haley's family home is now the ⊃**Alex Haley House Museum.**

Those stories inspired Haley to research his family members, who were brought to America as slaves, and the book came as a result. He recalls sitting on the front porch of his boyhood home and listening for hours to the stories.

Haley's museum by description is a "tribute to Kunta Kinte's worldwide family." Built in 1918 by a Kunta Kinte descendant, the house has been restored and not only serves as a tribute to Haley but also as a good example of rural small-town life in west Tennessee. It is also the first African-American state historic site and the only writer's home open to the public in Tennessee.

Following his death on February 10, 1992, Haley was buried in the front yard of the house, and his grave site is available for viewing at any time. Located at 200 South Church Street at Haley Avenue, the museum is open Tuesday through Sunday. Admission charged; (901) 738–2240.

In a bright red caboose in downtown Henning, the area's historical society has its records and artifacts on display in its heritage museum. Located on Main Street, adjacent to the city hall. If you'd like to visit, go into city hall and someone will come out and unlock the doors for you.

Crockett County

Crockett County was established in 1871 and named in honor of the famed Tennessee frontiersman Davy Crockett. The county seat of the 14,000 residents of the county is Alamo, where the *Crockett Times* newspaper has been published for more than 120 years. (901) 696–4558.

Crockett had already been killed when the county was formed, so when it came to finding a name for the new county, locals thought naming an entire county after the man would be an appropriate tribute. Cageville was renamed Alamo and became the county's center.

Crockett never lived in the county and there is no record that he ever visited here, but the people are proud of their living monument to one of the state's best-known sons.

Madison County

While many of his fellow craftspeople headed out to areas "where the tourists are," Larry Sellers settled on an area in the northern portion of the county near Medina, along Highway 45E. "I've been real surprised—I get a lot more tourists and out-of-state people in here than I ever dreamed I would."

114

Sellers is a wood carver and chain-saw artist and president of the ⊃**Tennessee Woods Art Gallery,** an outlet for his own and his friends' creations. A "born-again Baptist," Sellers decided to go into business for himself in 1984 with little more than faith in his "God-given" talent that he believed he had to use or lose. He is now one of the most sought-after artists in this part of the state.

As you pull up to the front of the gallery, a large, hollowed-out cypress log about 15 feet tall greets you. He makes these logs into unique treehouses. As you walk into the shop, a life-size Nativity scene attracts your attention. The twelve-piece set sells for about $9,000, and Sellers says he sells two or three a year. A large mountain man, which he says is slowly replacing the cigar-store Indian as the most popular wood carving, also greets you as you enter.

Sellers says the most requested item in his chain-saw line of art is the hillbilly figure, used almost exclusively as yard art. "It seems everybody wants a hillbilly in his front yard this year," he said. If you have a dead tree in your yard, he'll come out and carve a hillbilly for you out of its trunk for about $1,500. (901) 783–3265. Sellers' other business venture, the **Big Bad Wolf BBQ restaurant,** adjacent to the gallery, serves up some of the best barbecue in the area.

Farther south, in Jackson, construction on the city's first modern waterworks in the 1880s led to a discovery of one of the area's most prolific underground mineral water rivers. That powerful mineral spring, known as the **Electro Chalybeate Well,** still bubbles forth its clear waters. Through the years, thousands of people have come to its source searching for a cure for their internal ailments.

Shortly after the spring was discovered, a public park was developed around the spring and a lake was created. The area became quite an attraction for residents, and social life in the Jackson area soon revolved around the park. The park and the lake are both gone today, but a gazebo has been built over the remaining well, where people can still come to take the cure. The well is next to the city's restored art deco water plant, about three blocks from the town square on Royal Street, just south of the city's only remaining railroad station.

"Come all you rounders if you want to hear a story about a brave engineer." That's the beginning of the tale of Casey Jones, an engineer who became a legend after being killed in a much-publicized train crash. The ⊃**Casey Jones Home and Railroad Museum** tells the story of that fateful night. Casey was at the throttle of "Old 382" when it approached a stalled train on the same track near Vaughn, Mississippi, on April 30, 1900. The fireman jumped, and yelled to Casey to do the same, but instead he stayed on and valiantly tried to stop the train. He didn't succeed, but he slowed it down enough so that he was the only casualty of the wreck. The engineer immediately became a folk hero, and his story has been recounted for more than a half-century in story and song.

Casey was living in Jackson at the time of his death. His home has since been moved and now serves as the centerpiece of the museum, located in Jackson's Casey Jones Village on the Highway 45 By-Pass, just off Interstate 40. In addition to the museum, the village contains specialty shops and the **Brooks Shaw and Son Old Country Store,** a country restaurant complete with an 1880s-style soda fountain and large gift shop. Shops are free; admission is charged to the museum, which is open daily, year-round; (901) 668–1222.

Along historic Front Street in Henderson, Hugh Harville's two businesses are bringing worldwide attention to this small community. Known throughout the world for the soft plastic fishing lures he creates, the **Harville Manufacturing Co.** creates and ships out nearly five million lures a year.

Chester County

Three doors down from the factory, at 125 Front Street, his retail outlet, **Hugh's Tackle Box,** sells "several million" more lures, according to the entrepreneur. He invented the machines the lures are made on, and he not only sells his own brand but he also makes custom lures for other companies, who package them under their own brand names, and makes and ships out soft plastic lure parts for those who want to assemble their own lures.

Located in historic, pre-Civil War buildings, Harville has been in the business since the late 1960s. Due to insurance and security reasons, Hugh can't offer tours of his manufacturing plant, but if you stop by his retail store and he's around, he'll be happy to chat about fishing and, more specifically, about lures with you. Open Monday through Saturday, 8:00 A.M. to 4:30 P.M. (901) 989–5846.

Henderson County

Covering 43,000 acres, the Natchez Trace State Resort Park is Tennessee's largest state-run facility. It is also the home of the ↄ**"World's Third Largest Pecan Tree."** The tree is 106 feet tall, has a spread of 136 feet, and was planted in 1815. Legend says that one of General Andrew Jackson's men returning home from the Battle of New Orleans gave a pecan to a man called Sukey Morris, who then planted it because he didn't want to eat it.

The size of the tree is quite impressive, but what is more amazing is that the tree has been chronicled, by photos, almost since its "birth." Those photos are on display at the park's visitors center. The tree still gives a few pecans, but as one ranger said as she looked up at the tree, "It's hardly worth the effort to try and eat one. They aren't that good."

The massive park, with its lakes, trails, and heavily forested areas is a success story for one of President Roosevelt's New Deal programs. When the U.S. Department of Agriculture acquired the land in the early 1930s, the area was some of the most heavily abused and eroded land in the state. The area's occupants were relocated, and a "Land-Use Area" project was set up to demonstrate how wasteland could again be made productive through proper conservation practices.

Picturesque **Pin Oak Lodge and Restaurant,** situated in a heavily wooded area of the park next to a lake, offers some of the best food and lodging in this part of the state. Cabins, a swimming beach, family camping, off-road vehicle trails, fishing, boating, and miles of hiking are other attractions at the park. Open year-round; (901) 968–3742.

Decatur County

Each April coon hunters gather at the county fairgrounds just south of Parsons on Route 69 to take part in an event that is billed as the **"World's Largest Coon Hunt."** Depending on the year and the weather, about 600 hunters from thirty-five states come here to hunt for the state's "official" animal, the raccoon.

This is basically a competition for dogs, so no guns are allowed and no coons are hurt. The hunter with the dog who does the best "tracking and treeing" goes away as the winner. Since coons are nocturnal, most of the action on this weekend takes place at night. A country band plays until 3:00 A.M., and the local Jaycees keep their concession stands open around the clock for the entire weekend.

The event is considered to be the biggest independent fund raiser for St. Jude's Children's Research Hospital in Memphis. More than $100,000 is raised and donated each year.

Down along the banks of the Tennessee River, you'll find a fine little catfish restaurant called **Monroe's Tea Room.** With a large deck overlooking the river, the place is open April through Christmas and offers inside as well as outside eating. There are tasty steaks and burgers on the menu as well.

If you're coming by boat, it's at Mile Marker 140 on the river, and there's a gas pump and a small grocery store down on the banks for your use.

Open Wednesday through Sunday 4:00–11:00 P.M., except on Sunday when the grills heat up at noon. Take Highway 641 out of Decaturville and go 3 miles to Mount Carmel Road; the restaurant is on your left about 4 miles down Mount Carmel. (901) 852-3200.

If you're in the area on a Monday, make sure you drop by the **County Courthouse** in Decaturville. That's when the judges come to town for court. The circuit and juvenile courts are held each Monday, and there's usually a crowd gathered to watch the action. "It's a real big and busy day around here, especially if there's a murder trial going on," said one local observer.

Hardin County

The ↄ**Shiloh National Military Park and Cemetery,** 12 miles south of Savannah on Route 22, is a grim reminder of how bloody the Civil War really was.

On April 6 and 7, 1862, the North and South fought the first major battle in the western theater of the war here, just a few miles north of the Mississippi state line. More than 23,000 soldiers, about one-fourth of the total forces that fought, were casualties. The casualties in this one battle exceeded the total American casualties from the nation's three preceding wars, the Revolution, the War of 1812, and the Mexican War.

Known as Bloody Shiloh, the battle went down in the history books as one of the most gruesome in all American warfare. The park was established in 1894 and includes the battlefield and environs. A 9-mile self-guided auto tour highlights the battle and explains the various monuments that have been erected. The visitors center has a library and a museum, complete with relics and maps and a movie explaining the battle. Open daily, year-round; admission is charged; (901) 689–5275.

For a month prior to the Shiloh battle, the Union forces, under the leadership of General U.S. Grant, used the grounds of **Cherry Mansion,** 101 Main Street in nearby Savannah, as Union headquarters. Tents were set up in the yard, and Grant slept in the house and dined with the Cherry family. He was eating breakfast on April 6 when he got word of the battle of Shiloh.

Built in 1830, the house is the oldest structure in Savannah and is currently a private residence. The owner doesn't mind your taking pictures and looking at the exterior of the house, but please be considerate.

Six miles north of Savannah's city limits on Highway 128, in the small community of Cerro Gordo, is the **Harbour-Pitts store.** A huge brick building along the Tennessee River, the building was constructed in 1911. "My grandfather built the store to last," said Joe Pitts, the current owner and storekeep. The 9,000-square-foot store, with 24-foot-high ceilings, once had fourteen clerks on duty at one time. Now Joe can handle business by himself, with occasional help from his daughter.

To describe the store as anything but a hodge-podge of merchandise would be a disservice. Books, magazines, clothing, shoes, soda pop, guns, ammunition, and anything else you can think of line the shelves. Most of his business today comes from guns, hunting gear, and ammunition. On Tuesday nights there's a well-attended gun swap meeting, and during the winter they clean out the basement and set up a shooting range.

Although the merchandise displays look like mass confusion, Pitts assures a customer that it's not. "We've perfected the system," he said. "People like to hunt for things, and when they find something they like, they feel they've found something no one else knew was there."

Take a look at the well-worn stone stair as you walk in. It's a testament to the thousands who have visited the Pitts family business. Open Monday through Saturday, 7:00 A.M. to 6:00 P.M. (901) 925–4280.

About 2 miles farther north from Harbour-Pitts on Highway 128, take a left turn at the Saltillo Ferry sign and go down to the river. **Ferry Carolyn** is owned by Hardin County and runs Monday through Saturday, 6:00 A.M. to 5:00 P.M. For $1.00 you can take your car for a ride across the Tennessee River to Saltillo. Blow your horn if the ferry is on the other side.

Both Saltillo and Cerro Gordo were named after Mexican communities by soldiers returning to their Tennessee farmlands following the Mexican War. A brochure listing seventeen points of interest in Saltillo is available from city hall. After visiting some of the older homes and sites, make sure you stop by for a meal at **Vera's Country Kitchen.**

Located along historic Main Street, Vera's serves up a full line of meals, including her famous all-you-can-eat catfish platter. Open Tuesday through Sunday, 6:00 A.M. to 9:00 P.M. (901) 687–7242

McNairy County

The signs along Highway 64 outside Adamsville proclaim the community to be the "Biggest Little Town in Tennessee." A lot of that obvious pride may come from the fact that the town was home to one of America's most celebrated lawmen, Buford Pusser.

Pusser, who died in an auto accident in 1974, is immortalized today in the ⊃**Buford Pusser Home and Museum,** located at 342 Pusser Street. He was sheriff of this county from 1964 to 1970 and had the reputation of a no-nonsense, hard-nosed lawman. The exploits of this 6-foot, 6-inch tall, 250-pound "legend" were the basis of the three *Walking Tall* movies.

Today in the quiet residential area that he called home, his brick ranch house is overflowing with artifacts of his life. Following his death, his mother moved into the house and allowed nothing to be removed. Opened officially in 1988 as a museum, the facility is owned and operated by the city. Everything from his credit cards to his toothbrush to the roll of $100 bills he had in his pocket when he was killed are on display. An advertisement from a mattress company rests on his bed. "Big Buford Bedding, designed to honor a man who walked tall in Tennessee."

The years he spent as sheriff were hard ones on this "soft-spoken country gentleman." He was shot eight times, knifed seven times, and gunned down in an ambush that killed his wife. Many residents feel the flaming auto crash that took his life was no accident.

According to the museum's hostess, Jimmie Powers, Pusser was constantly on guard and often remarked that he was "on borrowed time." His home is a reflection of that attitude. He had a special entrance built on the lower level, where his underground bedroom and living quarters were. He slept with his head against the earthen wall to help protect himself against the continuous threats.

In addition to his personal belongings, numerous scrapbooks of newspaper clippings, a videotape of television interviews, and a copy of his 1956 high school yearbook are on display. Admission charged; (901) 632–4080.

Up Highway 224 near Leapwood, the **Coon Creek Science Center** reveals that this whole area was under a sea about 70 million years ago. The center, opened in late 1989, is owned and operated by the Memphis Museum System, although it is more than 100 miles from that city.

When emptied, the warm, shallow ocean left behind an abundance of unusual and significant geological treasures. The marine shells found here in the bottomlands are not actually fossils but the real things, since they have not undergone the process of mineralization and have not turned to stone. The clay of the area has preserved the shells in their original form.

Known as the Coon Creek fossil formation, the entire area attracts geologists from all over the world. The center has been established to preserve the area and to provide an educational facility for the study of the earth sciences.

Various educational exhibits and programs have been established and are available for groups of fifteen or more. If you're not in a specific group and want to see the place, the center sponsors several "family days" during the year when individuals can sign up for a program. The Jackson Parks and Recreation Department (901–427–6724) also has several programs a year here that individuals may sign up for. (901) 632–4850.

The hog is king at **Pappy Johns** whole hog barbecue, located on Highway 45 South, a few miles outside Selmer. Here, you gotta be hungry for pork, because that's the only meat served. Open daily except Sunday, pork ribs are cooked up three nights a week, Wednesday, Friday, and Saturday, while the rest of the hog is available all the other times. A good deal of the business here is take-out, but if you enjoy eating near the hickory pits where the cooking is done, there are tables inside. (901) 645–4353.

Less than a mile down the road from Pappy Johns is the sprawling **Kings Antiques.** Located in more buildings and sheds than you can count from the road, Kings' sign says that it has more than 15,000 items and that it sells used cars and appliances as well as antiques and collectibles. It also offers small-engine repair. Open daily except Sunday and Monday.

Along Highway 57 just east of Ramer city limits, you'll find a nice piece of folk art in the Deming family's front yard. A tall bicycle sculpture made out of old wagon wheels and various other pieces of "junk," the item is a true piece of roadside Americana.

Hardeman County

The county's first courthouse, now known as the ↄ**Little Courthouse,** was built in 1824, making it one of the oldest original courthouses in western Tennessee. Located at 116 East Market Street in Bolivar, the restored structure now houses the county museum.

The original part of the existing building was a two-story log structure that served as the courthouse. In 1827 the building was purchased and moved to its current site, where additions were made to the log structure. It was converted into a family residence in 1849 and more additions were made, turning it into a large Federal-style home.

The building itself is worth the stop, but some of the items inside highlighting this county are fascinating in themselves. Open by appointment or by chance; admission charged; (901) 658–6554.

Another historic structure in Bolivar is the **The Pillars,** former home of John Houston Bills, one of the original settlers of West Tennessee. Built prior to 1826, the building saw the likes of James K. Polk, Davy Crockett, General U.S. Grant, and Sam

Houston. Open by appointment or chance; admission charged; (901) 658–6554.

The **Magnolia Manor** is this area's premier bed and breakfast. The 1849 structure has been completely restored to its early splendor with wooden floors throughout. Owners James and Elaine Cox currently run the three-guest-room inn. Rates to stay at the antebellum inn range from $55 to $65, including a choice of meals. In the hallway you'll find portraits of four famous generals who stayed here many years before you found out about the place. Commissioned by the Cox family, the portraits feature U. S. Grant, William T. Sherman, John A. Logan, and James B. McPherson. Located at 418 North Main Street; (901) 658–6700.

The **Anderson Fruit Farm** is considered the state's largest orchard. Covering 250 acres near Cloverport, the farm has more than 25,000 apple, peach, and pear trees in an area better known for its cotton production than fruit.

In addition, corn, peas, sweet potatoes, tomatoes, squash, okra, green beans, melons, and blackberries are all raised here and sold in season. More than 10,000 gallons of apple cider are made and sold each year.

Visitors can pick their own peaches and apples during the proper seasons, with rides to the orchards provided on a hay wagon. The Andersons welcome guests to their orchards, on Highway 138 in Toone, but their fruit and produce are also available at their roadside market in nearby Whiteville. (901) 658–5524.

Quail hunting is a big sport in the southern part of the county. Sporting clubs specializing in quail hunting are dotted across the bottom part of the state. Not relying on Mother Nature, owners of these clubs buy quail and release a certain number in a field for their paying customers.

One of the bird suppliers is the ꓛ**Flying Feathers Quail Farm,** just south of Highway 57 near Saulsbury. More than one covey of quail can be found here at Joe Jordan's bird farm. He specializes in American bob whites and admits that it can be quite noisy around the farm at times.

"It's my job to raise a bird that is as close to a wild bird as possible," claims Jordan as he carefully walks among the young chicks. Once the chicks are old enough, he puts them in a fly pen where he encourages them to learn to fly. The 50-foot by 120-foot fly pen is crucial to their "wild bird" education.

The birds are sold to the preserves when they are about

fourteen to sixteen weeks old. Jordan will take you on a tour of this facility. Call for directions; (901) 764–2950.

About 7 miles west on Highway 57 is the small community of Grand Junction, home of the **National Field Trial Champ-ionships.** Held at the 18,600-acre Ames Plantation since 1896, the annual February event is often called the "Super Bowl of Bird Dogs."

Competition lasts eight to ten days, with the winning dog earning the title of World Champion Bird Dog. Hunting mostly for quail, the dogs and handlers are followed by a large gallery of spectators on horseback. As quail raiser Joe Jordan says about the mounted spectators: "There must be 4,000 or 5,000 of them out there at a time. They never see a dog, but they sure have a good time."

The plantation, although synonymous with the quest for canine excellence, plays an integral part in the University of Tennessee's livestock and agriculture program. The facility is one of the eleven branch experiment stations in the university's system. Built in 1847, the **Ames Manor House** is open to the public on the fourth Thursday afternoon of each month from March through October. $2.00 admission charge; (901) 878–1067.

While Ames Plantation is the official headquarters, **Dunn's Supply Company** in downtown Grand Junction is the gathering place for local as well as international bird-dog aficionados. The store carries just about anything one would need for bird hunting and other outdoor activities. (901) 764–6901.

Across the street from Dunn's is the **Field Trial Hall of Fame and National Wildlife Heritage Center.** Created by the Bird Dog Foundation, the dedication plaque reads: "Dedicated to preserving the past, protecting the future for sporting dog fanciers the world over."

Films, paintings of some of the most famous bird dogs of the past hundred years, artifacts, literature, photography, and other memorabilia are featured here and help tell the story of the talents of well-trained bird dogs. If you're not familiar with any of this, don't worry; the folks working here are more than eager to share their love of the sport and of the dogs with you. Admission charged; (901) 764–2058.

Over at 133 Madison Avenue in Grand Junction, you'll find a real gem. The **Tennessee Pewter Showroom** is the only commercial producer of a full line of pewter products in the south.

Pewtersmith Carl Dunn uses both the spin and the cast method of production to make all kinds of things ranging from beer steins to sugar bowls to pitchers to dinner plates. In all, he and the other craftsmen make about 135 different items.

The showroom is open Monday through Friday 9:00 A.M. to 4:00 P.M., but if you want to see Dunn in action, you'll have to show up between 7:30 A.M. and 4:00 P.M. on Tuesday or Wednesday. Those are the days he's most apt to be casting and spinning the molten pewter. (901) 764–2064.

Fayette County

Heading toward Memphis on Highway 57, you'll find ⊃**LaGrange,** a quaint little village that has been able to avoid the commercialization that the others have fallen to along this busy highway corridor. In addition to a couple of antique shops, the streets are lined with a plethora of well-kept little white cottages with green shutters and trim. Settled in 1819 on the site of an Indian trading post, it was named for General Lafayette's ancestral home in France. Translated to mean "beautiful village," it was occupied by Union forces from 1862 to 1865. It was an antebellum center of wealth, education, and culture, having had two colleges, four academies, two newspapers, and 3,000 residents in 1862.

Tipton County

In Mason, just across the county line on Highway 70, is ⊃**Bozo's Restaurant.** Look for one of those tiled cafe buildings that dotted America's landscape a while back, and you'll find Bozo's.

Founded in 1923 by Bozo Williams, the restaurant has stayed in the family and is now owned by the founder's great-grandson, Jeff Thompson. Famous for its pork shoulder barbecue sandwiches and plates, Bozo's has a full menu that has not changed since shortly after World War II.

When he took over ownership in 1988, Thompson was told by "just about everybody" not to change a thing. One thing he did do, however, was to bottle and sell the establishment's popular sauces. Food comes with no sauce, allowing the diner to choose between the hot and mild concoctions located on each table.

Having never advertised, the restaurant's one-hundred seats are filled by longtime customers and newcomers who have heard about the place from a friend. On weekends about 50 percent of the business comes from Memphis, 35 miles away. Bozo's is open Monday through Saturday from 10:30 A.M. to 9:00 P.M. and offers the same menu items all day; (901) 294-3400.

Shelby County

With a population of about 700,000, Memphis rests along the Mississippi River and is one of the river's largest inland ports. Among many other things, the city is famous for its impact on the development of popular American music as well as the blues.

The history of music in the Memphis area revolves around the "King of Rock and Roll," Elvis Presley. Although he died in 1977, Elvis is more popular today than when he was alive; and his estate is worth much more now ($75 million) than it was when he died ($4.9 million) because of his home (Graceland Mansion), souvenir and tourist shops, and museums. Estate revenues were topping $15 million by the late 1980s, more than the singer made in any one year of his career.

⊃**Graceland Mansion,** at 3765 Elvis Presley Boulevard, is one of the many unique places in the state where the beaten path catches up with the unbeaten path. There's nothing like this anywhere in the world, and it shouldn't be missed. Elvis and his family are buried here in the Meditation Garden, and tours of the mansion are run daily, year-round, except for Christmas, Thanksgiving, and New Year's Day. Closed Tuesdays in November and December.

You'll get a chance to walk the grounds, see his private recording studio, tour his bus and his private jet, the *Lisa Marie,* named after his daughter. You'll also have the opportunity to add to his estate at a variety of merchandise shops across the street from the mansion. It would be a good idea to make reservations, because the lines can get very long, especially during the summer months. Admission charged; (901) 332-3322.

Each year in mid-August Memphis hosts the Elvis International Tribute Week, an action-packed week of events that includes trivia contests, candelight vigils, special tours, tournaments, and parties. Humes Junior High School, where Elvis graduated from in 1953, is also open for tours and features a special exhibit room and a chance to walk across the stage where Elvis performed in a talent show.

Sun Studios, where Elvis recorded a song for his mother for $4.00, is open to the public. Founded by disc jockey Sam Phillips, Sun was the first studio to record such musicians as Presley, Jerry Lee Lewis, Carl Perkins, and Johnny Cash. The studio is located at 706 Union Avenue, just a few blocks from Baptist Hospital, where Elvis was pronounced dead on August 16, 1977. Open seven days a week, with tours scheduled every hour on the half-hour from 9:30 a.m. to 5:00 p.m. Admission charged; (901) 521–0664.

つ**Beale Street,** in downtown Memphis, is considered the spiritual home of the other type of music the city is famous for, the blues. During its heyday in the twenties and thirties, there wasn't a tougher, more swinging street in America. The zoot suit originated here, and Machine Gun Kelly peddled bootleg on the streets. Always a mecca for musicians, the street's nightclubs were frequented by the country's best blues artists, including the man known as the Father of the Blues, the legendary William Christopher (W.C.) Handy.

Today the street is once again a hot nightspot with numerous clubs, restaurants, and shops. And the best part is that the sound of the blues has not been forgotten. Four clubs now offer traditional blues and jazz music: **Mr. Handy's Blues Hall** at 174 Beale; the **Rum Boogie Cafe** at 182 Beale; **B.B. King's Blues Club,** at 147 Beale; and **Joyce Cobb's** club at 203 Beale.

Virtually unchanged through the years is **Schwab's** dry goods store, where a sign still hangs in the window proclaiming "If you can't find it here, you're better off without it." The clerks still offer old-time service with a written receipt for each item purchased.

Downstairs, the Schwab family has created a museum. Having been on Beale Street since 1876, they have been able to collect quite a few memories of the "good ole days" to display. Upstairs, the store sells all sorts of items, from dream books to straw sailors to crystal balls to size 74 men's pants. Forty-four kinds of suspenders are kept in stock.

The **Memphis Police Museum** is located at 159 Beale Street. It's located in an active police substation and is open every day, all day, all night. This precinct currently houses the walking, bicycle, and horse details for the Beale Street and downtown areas of the city.

Among other items, the museum has on tape the first car-to-car radio broadcast that took place in the city in 1940. Elvis also is saluted here. He was a reserve police captain, and the picture of him and his chief along with special orders taking him off the roll call following his death are on display, as are other Elvis-police-related memorabilia. Admission free; (901) 528–2370.

After wining and dining on Beale Street, head out to the airport, where one of the most interesting industrial tours in the country begins weeknights at 11:30. Federal Express has its major hub here, and during the hour and a half that it will take you to walk through the facilities, jets will bring in more than 400,000 packages while 2,800 employees help sort them out and direct them in the right direction. Twenty-three miles of high-speed conveyer belts are used in the operation. (901) 369–3600.

If it's history you came to Memphis for, take the short trip out to ⊃**Mud Island,** out in the Mississippi River across from downtown. The city has developed this area to display its rich river heritage. The River Walk is a five-block-long scale model of the entire Lower Mississippi's 1,000 miles from Cairo, Illinois, to the Gulf of Mexico. Every twist, turn, and split the river makes is shown on the model. Each step equals 1 mile along the miniriver, where each bridge and town is also depicted. Markers along the way point out interesting facts and figures. Water flows down the model into a one-acre Gulf of Mexico.

In 1989 sand was added to the 4-foot-deep gulf and Boogie Beach was created. Now open for swimming, it's the largest swimming pool in the city.

The eighteen-gallery **Mississippi River Museum** is also located on the island and is a showcase for the people and the history of the river, with exhibits ranging from Indian arrowheads to a replica of the pilot house of a modern diesel towboat.

One of the galleries traces the wreck of the steamboat *Sultana,* which burned and sank nearby, killing 1,547 people. It is considered the worst maritime disaster in United States history. (901) 576–7241.

A visit to the ⊃**Peabody Hotel,** at 149 Union Street in downtown, is a must. Built in 1925, the grand hotel has been restored and carries on a tradition started back in the mid-thirties. Each

The Peabody Ducks

morning at eleven o'clock, five ducks are transported by elevator from their penthouse facilities to the lobby of the hotel.

As the doors slowly open, a red carpet is unrolled from the big fountain to the elevator as the "King Cotton March" is played over the sound system. With ranks of attending bellmen along both sides of the carpet, the ducks waddle to the fountain where they will spend the day. At 5:00 P.M., the action is reversed, and the ducks go back to their duck palace on the roof.

The palace is open to visitors, but that's not all you'll find up there. You'll also find a very impressive view of the river and downtown Memphis. (901) 529–4000.

Metalsmithing, everything from delicate gold jewelry to massive wrought-iron fencing, is the subject of one of the area's most unusual museums. Located in downtown Memphis on a bluff overlooking the Mississippi River, the **National Ornamental Metal Museum** was opened to the public in 1979 as a memorial to metalsmithing.

Changing exhibits are the basis of the museum, but its permanent collection contains a variety of items from jewelry to handmade nails to large outdoor sculptures to ancient iron locks. In the museum's smithy (anyplace where metal is worked) work is done daily by resident artists and members of museum classes. On the third weekend of October each year, "Repair Days" is held. People from all over the South bring in their broken metal items to be fixed. On an average, sixty craftspeople are available during that time to repair "broken, bent or otherwise mutilated metalwork."

The museum grounds, at 374 West California, are a part of what was once known as the Marine Hospital, with the oldest of the three large brick buildings dating from 1870. That building was used in the extensive Memphis research that led to a cure for the yellow fever epidemics that once swept the area. The museum's main exhibit building was built as a Works Progress Administration project in 1932 and once served as a nurse's dormitory for the hospital complex. Admission charged; (901) 774–6380.

Remember when you had to drive out West to get Coors beer? Well, those days came to an end when the company started shipping their brew east of the Mississippi in 1981. First, they opened a brewery in Shenandoah, Virginia; then, in September 1991, the **Memphis Brewery** opened in the old Joseph Schlitz Brewery.

Retrofitting is about finished, and this facility now brews, bottles or cans, and ships Coors Cutters, a nonalcoholic beer. Coors and Coors Light are brewed in Golden, Colorado, and shipped to Memphis in refrigerated tanker cars. Upon arrival here those products are canned or bottled and shipped.

There are three can lines in operation, each filling up to 1,600 cans per minute. Two bottle lines are also in use. Free tours are given Monday through Saturday, every half-hour, from 10:00 A.M. to 4:00 P.M. During the thirty-minute trek you'll be briefed on the history of the brewery and you'll get to see all facets of the operation. The tour ends in the Belle Hospitality Center, where you'll get to sample the great Coors products. The brewery is at 5151 East Raines Road; (901) 375–2100 or (901) 368–BEER.

Of all the sites listed in this guide, the one that seems most out of place in Tennessee is the magnificent **Pyramid,** located in Memphis along the banks of the Mississippi River. The 32-story-tall stainless steel structure, built in the shape of a pyramid, opened to the public in late 1991. It is currently the home of a 20,000-seat arena where concerts, sporting events, and ice shows take place.

From the floor of the arena you can look straight up 321 feet to the top floor, which will become a glass-enclosed observation deck in the future. A glass-enclosed incline elevator will take guests up the outside of the building to the deck. In addition, there is 180,000 square feet of space in the four corners of the building that will be developed into museums, restaurants, and other attractions.

Guided tours start on the Plaza Level and are conducted Monday through Saturday, 10:00 A.M. to 4:00 P.M., and on Sunday, noon to 4:00 P.M. Admission charged. One Auction Avenue; (901) 521–9675.

INDEX

Index

Index

Acknowledgments

It's amazing how many people know so much, and it sure was nice that they all wanted to share that knowledge with a stranger.

As I drove the blue-line highways of the state of Tennessee searching for off-the-beaten-path sorts of things, I stopped and talked to many people, and to the best of my recollection each one I approached was able to help me in some fashion. It was from these people that I discovered many of the items in this book, and I thank them for their Southern hospitality.

I also wish to thank each and every employee of every chamber of commerce and tourism office I stopped at requesting information. They furnished a plethora of insightful local color.

When people are willing to share their knowledge with others, it makes a job a lot easier. I couldn't have done it without a lot of help. Thanks to everyone!

About the Author

Tim O'Brien is a veteran news reporter and editor who now travels the world's highways for a living as Southeast editor for *Amusement Business Newsweekly*. His specialty area of reportage is amusement parks and other types of tourist attractions.

When he's not traveling, he's at his home base near Nashville, Tennessee, where he lives with his wife, Rosi, and daughters, Carrie and Molly.

A graduate of Ohio State University with a Masters degree in Journalism/Film Production, Tim is also an accomplished photographer and a roller coaster fanatic, having ridden many of the world's greatest coasters.

He has written two other Globe Pequot books: *The Amusement Park Guide* and *Where the Animals Are*.

United States Travel

Here are some other fine guides from our *Off the Beaten Path* series designed for the traveler who enjoys the special and unusual. Each book is by an author who knows the state well, did extensive research, and personally visited many of the places, often more than once. Please check your local bookstore for other fine Globe Pequot Press titles which include:

Alabama, $9.95
Arkansas, $9.95
Colorado, $9.95
Connecticut, $9.95
Florida, $8.95
Georgia, $9.95
Hawaii, $10.95
Illinois, $9.95
Indiana, $9.95
Iowa, $9.95
Kansas, $9.95
Kentucky, $9.95
Louisiana, $8.95
Maine, $9.95
Maryland, $9.95
Massachusetts, $9.95
Michigan, $9.95

Minnesota, $9.95
Missouri, $9.95
Montana, $9.95
New Hampshire, $9.95
New Jersey, $9.95
New Mexico, $9.95
New York, $8.95
North Carolina, $9.95
Northern California, $9.95
Ohio, $9.95
Oregon, $9.95
Pennsylvania, $9.95
Southern California, $8.95
Virginia, $9.95
Washington, $9.95
Wisconsin, $9.95

To order any of these titles with MASTERCARD or VISA, call toll-free 1–800–243–0495, in Connecticut call 1–800–962–0973. Free shipping for orders of three or more books. Shipping charge of $3.00 per book for one or two books ordered. Connecticut residents add sales tax. Ask for your free catalogue of Globe Pequot's quality books on recreation, travel, nature, gardening, cooking, crafts, and more. Prices and availability subject to change.